A KENDAL SKETCHBOOK

A KENDAL SKETCHBOOK

by Michael Bottomley

Published in 2008 by
Kendal Civic Society
in conjunction with
E.M. Bottomley.

ISBN 978-0-9509869-5-1

Designed and printed by
Titus Wilson and Son, Kendal.

Kendal Town Hall from Fellside
pen and ink 1967
39 x 27

Frontispiece:
Waterside

Title page:
Kendal Castle
pencil drawing 1986

CONTENTS

Staircase projection at the rear of
No. 112 Stricklandgate
pencil drawing 1952
20 x 12

PREFACE

Kendal has been the centre of my working life and I have been sketching and painting in the town since 1947. Made over a period of fifty years the images included in this book record many aspects of the town during the latter half of the twentieth century. Some of the buildings and views will be familiar today, others will evoke memories of the past. Some were made because it was clear that the buildings would soon be gone but most of them were drawn or painted because I enjoyed their picturesque qualities.

It is primarily a book of pictures but historical notes have been added on most pages. The paintings have been arranged on a topographical basis so that the book could illustrate a walk round the town.

The route commences with Stricklandgate where there has been much recent re-development. It continues along Highgate taking in Lowther Street and some of the yards. A climb up Collin Croft and Beast Banks to Cliff Terrace is followed by a descent through Fellside. A walk down Stramongate reveals long lost views of crumbling yards. This is followed by a stroll along the river with its industrial associations, and finishes in Kirkland. Finally there is a group of paintings 'from my window' high above Lowther Street.

It was thought that the inclusion of a map would help those not familiar with the town and provide a useful reference point for all. But which map to use? An up to date one would not show the location of the buildings which have been demolished during these decades, so it was decided to use the 1853 'Plan of Kendal' by Henry Hoggarth, a local surveyor of the time.

Miller Bridge
pencil drawing 1978
23 x 15

ACKNOWLEDGEMENTS

I am extremely grateful to all those who have helped me in compiling this book. Firstly to those friends who have allowed me to reproduce paintings from their own collections – to Alan Elvey, Ron Gerrard, Roger Haigh, Adam Naylor, Milne Moser, Austen Robinson.

Secondly to Titus Wilson and Son, my printers, especially David Pointon and Bryan Harper whose expertise has been invaluable and with whom it has been a pleasure to work. Thanks also to Janet Martin for her meticulous proof-reading.

My biggest debt of gratitude is to Diane and Roger Haigh without whose persistent encouragement and advice together with that of their families there would have been no book.

ILLUSTRATIONS

Wherever possible the reproductions of paintings and drawings have been dated and the size of the original given in centimetres, height before width.
(private collection) indicates that the original has been borrowed for reproduction.

1 STRICKLANDGATE

This chapter follows Stricklandgate from the top of Finkle Street, taking in the Market Place and the west side of the street where there has been considerable rebuilding during the last 50 years.

Kendal Market
pencil sketch 1958
12 x 20

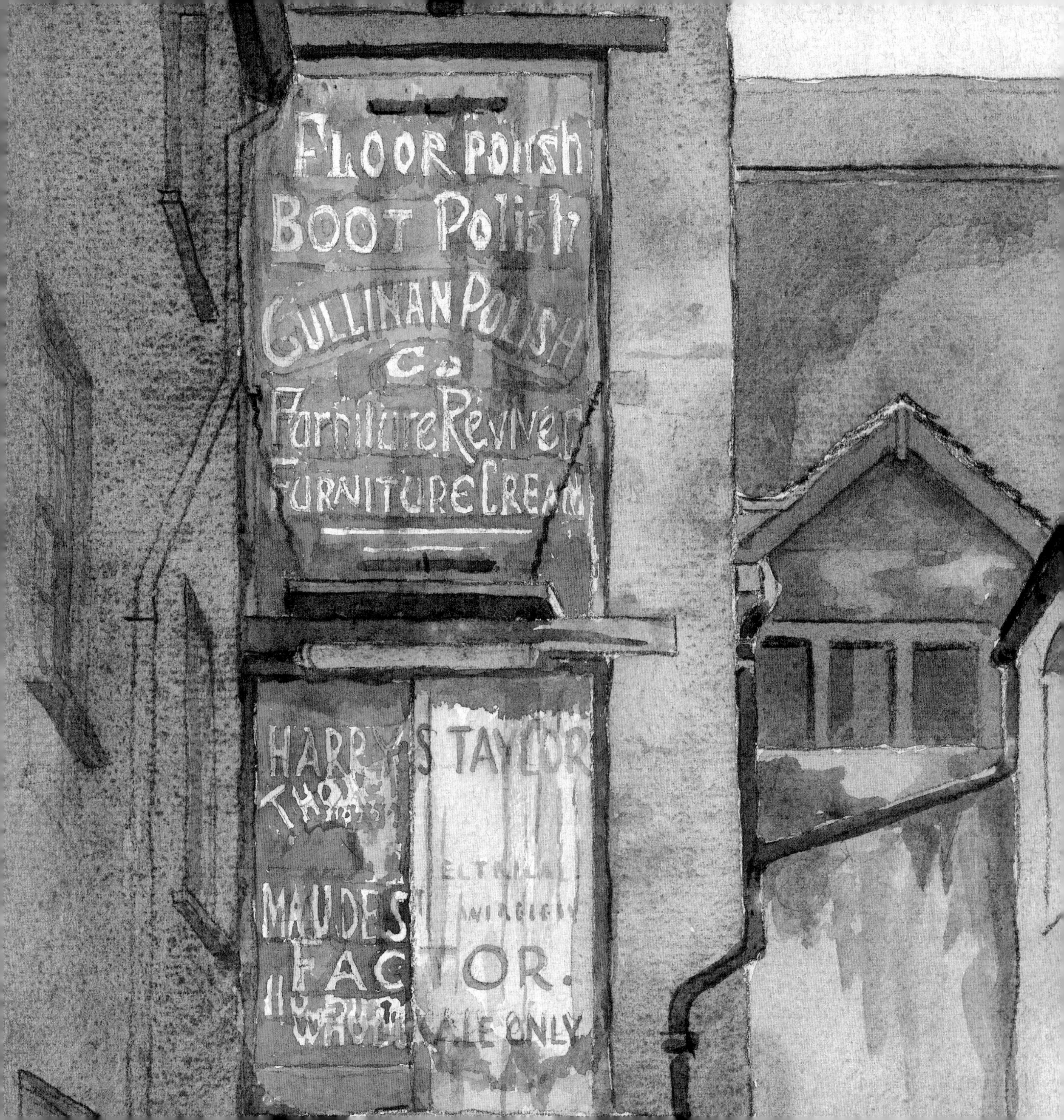

FLOOR POLISH
BOOT POLISH
CULLINAN POLISH
Co
Furniture Reviver
FURNITURE CREAM
HARRY S TAYLOR
MAUDES
FACTOR.
WHOL ALE ONLY

Farrer's Tea Mart and Coffee Warehouse
No. 13 Stricklandgate
watercolour 1947
36 x 25

Nos. 13-19 Stricklandgate form a continuous row of lath and plaster fronted houses of which only Farrer's retains its original shop front. The others were fitted with new shop fronts about 1880. Inside the shop many of its original fittings are retained.

In 1947 coffee was still roasted on the top floor, hence the open windows and stove pipe protruding from the roof – delightful mouth-watering aromas used to waft across the street.

Kendal Market
pastel 1958
37 x 48
(private collection)

Kendal's first charter to hold a market on Saturdays was granted in 1189 by Richard I.

The north side of the Market Place, shown here, has changed little in the last 50 years, except that the Globe Inn, originally with a timber, lath and plaster front, has been rebuilt in blockwork. The War Memorial is just out of sight towards the left.

The New Shambles
watercolour and gouache 1995
26 x 18
(private collection)

The New Shambles was built in 1803 for the butchers, because the sloping site offered better drainage than the Old Shambles off Highgate.

Nos 34-46 Stricklandgate
pen, ink and watercolour 1951
29 x 38

These buildings faced the Market Place on the opposite side of Stricklandgate. In the centre are the two gables of the former White Lion Inn.
The shop fronts replaced a two storey gallered façade about 1890. Townley & Taylor sold toys and prams and were local agents for Meccano sets and Hornby trains.

Immmediately to the left is the former Rose and Crown Inn which by 1950 had become a branch of the Scotch Wool Shop.
The four storey bulding to the right was owned by J. Bird who sold hardware, boots and shoes, etc. It is now a branch of W. H. Smith. The buildings in the centre have been demolished and rebuilt twice since 1951.

White Lion Yard
pen, ink and watercolour 1951
31 x 24

The opening between the premises of Townley & Taylor and those of J. Bird led to White Lion Yard with its view up to Fellside.

White Lion Yard
pen, ink and watercolour 1952
31 x 24

Looking east to the back of Townley & Taylor's and showing the close proximity of houses on the right to warehouses on the left with loading doors at first floor level.

Entry Lane
pen, ink and watercolour 1950
31 x 23

Entry Lane is an ancient highway leading from the town centre to Low Fellside and Kendal Fell.
The buildings to the right were a joiner's workshop in 1950 but have since been demolished.

Elephant Yard
pen, ink and watercolour 1959
28 x 39

Thomas Sandes, one of Kendal's wealthy merchants, built his 'house of manufacture, schoolroom and library' here in 1659. Much of that building was replaced in 1820 by the Elephant Inn. Thomas Sandes (1606-1681) was the founder of the Sandes Hospital almshouses and the Bluecoat School, later amalgamated with the Grammar School.

This picture shows the first court of the yard with a cottage in which some oak panelling dated TSK 1651 (for Thomas and Katherine Sandes) survived until it was demolished in 1959. The panelling was rescued and is now in the Abbot Hall Museum of Lakeland Life and Industry.

Dick Ashburn's Smithy
pen, ink and watercolour 1951
22 x 31

Further up Elephant Yard was a smithy occupied by Dick Ashburn, the last of a long line of blacksmiths, whitesmiths and wheelwrights on this site.

The smithy and other buildings in the yard were demolished to make way for extensions to the Woolpack Inn and a car park. These in turn were demolished and the site re-developed as the Elephant Yard Shopping Centre in 1999.

Fellside from Library Road
pen, ink and watercolour 1952
27 x 38

In the foreground is the entrance to Webb's nursery garden, later developed as a supermarket and car park (now Marks and Spencer).
The roofs of All Hallows church and Job Pennington's chapel can be recognised beyond and on the skyline to the left is Cliff Terrace.

Much of Fellside was rebuilt in the 50s and 60s but some of the old buildings can be seen today.

No. 45 and Yard 47 Stricklandgate
pen and watercolour 1949
37 x 28

These buildings, already empty in 1949, were soon after demolished to create a car park. The Westmorland Shopping Centre was eventually built on the site. Briggs' shoe shop moved across the road where it continued for many years.

Yard 110 Stricklandgate
watercolour 1994
42 x 27

Harry S. Taylor of Whitehaven were wholesalers and motor factors with a Kendal branch in Maude Street. This entrance from a yard in Stricklandgate had typical loading doors and platforms to upper floors with a hoist above. The warehouse has been replaced by an apartment block.

2 HIGHGATE

In Highgate were the houses of some of Kendal's principal inhabitants. The long plots of land behind them ran down to the river on the east side and climbed to Garth Heads on the west. These plots were gradually built up with workshops and cottages and became known as yards.

Dr Manning's Yard
pen and ink

Dr Manning practised from this yard in the early 20th century. It was formerly known as Braithwaite's Yard after George Braithwaite, dyer and drysalter, who lived at the top of the yard and had his dye house and woollen mill towards the river.

New Bank Yard
watercolour 1952
37 x 48
(private collection)

New Bank Yard was one of the most attractive and well preserved of the Kendal yards. Running from Highgate next to Martins Bank (now Barclays) to the New Road opposite Miller Bridge, it featured several houses built across the yard with external access stairs.

This house at the east end of the yard is the only building to survive when New Bank Yard together with the two yards on either side of it were demolished by Kendal Borough Council to create a car park.

New Bank Yard
watercolour 1952
35 x 38

Kendal Civic Society campaigned for the preservation of New Bank Yard and prepared a plan for retaining and restoring the best buildings and providing car parking spaces on the perimeter. This was rejected by the council and demolition went ahead.

Some years later, following local government re-organisation, South Lakeland House and the adjoining multi-storey car park were built over most of the site.

The Angel Inn
watercolour and gouache 1983-5
25 x 18

The Angel Inn is remarkable for its row of chimneys set diagonally along the roof ridge and the central box-like construction said to be a cock pit where illicit cock fighting 'mains' could be patronised.

The building has been partly rebuilt and is now a branch of the Halifax Building Society.
The open shed has gone but the elder tree in the foreground is still there providing an excellent feature at the entrance to South Lakeland House.

No. 27 Lowther Street
watercolour 1948
37 x 25

Lowther Street was formed in 1782. Gawith, Hoggarth & Company, tobacco and snuff manufacturers, established their business at No. 27 in 1887.

The painting shows the original 'Turk' trade sign, which collapsed in 1973 and was replaced by a replica.

Rear of No. 29 Lowther Street
watercolour 1949
38 x 32

No. 29 Lowther Street was the home of Samuel Gawith, Mayor of Kendal who died in 1865. It became the family house of the Hoggarths who also refurbished No. 31.

Before Gulfs Road was formed the garden of No. 29 extended down to the river and included a summer house, now absorbed into the offices and café on Waterside.
The garden had become rather derelict when this drawing was made. Behind the greenhouse can be seen the chimney of the snuff works next door.

Kendal Roofscape
pen, ink and watercolour 1959
28 x 32

This view from the rear of No. 35 Highgate shows the backs of the buildings on the south side of Lowther Street with their small yards, the former chimney of Gawith, Hoggarth's snuff works and in the distance Benson Knott.

Nos. 53-59 Highgate
pen, ink and watercolour 1952
28 x 37
(private collection)

These buildings were erected by Samuel Gawith in 1861, perhaps to commemorate his mayoralty in that year. They were designed by Stephen Shaw.

Note that Highgate was still a two way street in 1952.
For many years No. 59 was occupied by Milne Moser & Son, solicitors, whose brass plate, polished daily, was so worn as to be almost illegible.

Yard 57 Highgate
pen, ink and pastel 1952
33 x 28

Here we see the rear of Nos. 53-59 with a single storey range of offices.

Yard 77 Highgate
watercolour 1973
38 x 27

The yard has changed little since the painting was made.

To the right are the backs of the houses in Dr Manning's Yard.

Yard 119 Highgate
pen, ink, watercolour and chalk 1962
30 x 24

This yard, like most of those on the east side of Highgate, provided a way down to the waterside. At the bottom of the yard was the workshop of P. Bland, tinsmith and sheet metalworker.

The Oddfellows' Hall
pen, ink and watercolour 1950
30 x 36

The Oddfellows' Hall was built in 1833 to the design of George Webster. In 1857 it was occupied by the Mechanics' Institute and later the YMCA. After various other uses it has recently become apartments.

Note the gas light – gas lighting was introduced to Kendal in 1825 but as late as 1950, the main streets of the town were still illuminated by gas, the lamps being lit every evening by a lamplighter with a pole.

No. 163 Highgate
watercolour 1948
33 x 28

The prominent shop with its entrance on the corner was occupied by Sedgwick's butchers when this painting was made. It had previously been a grocer's shop and before that a chemist's.

On the right at No. 167 a queue is forming at Hanratty's fish and chip shop.

The Brewery
pen, ink and watercolour 1951
28 x 38

This house was built by a member of the Wilson Family of Dallam Tower. The arms of Wilson impaling those of Crowle are still to be seen on the lead spout head.
Whitwell, Mark & Co. established their wine business in 1757. In 1853 their new brewery was built over the garden at the rear of this house.

The panelled dining room was converted into an office and later a new pedimented doorway inserted. The original entrance in typical Kendal fashion had been from the yard entry at the side.
The much altered and enlarged brewery premises at the rear have now become the Brewery Arts Centre. The former offices are a Youth Hostel.

West Side of Highgate
pen, ink and watercolour 1951
28 x 38

From the left we see the Shakespeare Inn with its semi-basement shops, built in 1830, a year after the Shakespeare Theatre was opened at the head of the yard. The pleasant house next door has now become a shop.
The imposing limestone building to the right was built as the Bank of Westmorland to the design of George Webster in 1834.

The bank had been founded the year before as a joint stock company in competition with the two private banks which had been in existence since 1788. The bank was taken over by the Midland Bank in 1893 and is now part of HSBC. The front door, steps and railings were altered in 1966.
To the left of the bank is the entrance to Collin Croft.

3 FELLSIDE

The area known as Fellside lies between Low Fellside and Serpentine Road but I have included in this section Collin Croft for its obvious picturesque qualities. Also included are Monument House and Cliff Terrace which show aspects of the town's development in the early nineteenth century.

Fellside from Bowling Fell
pencil drawing 1960
22 x 37

The Old Shambles
pen, conté and watercolour 1950
27 x 23

The drawing shows the abrupt way in which the Fellside rises above the head of the yards off the east side of Highgate.

The Shambles was built in 1779 to accommodate the town's butchers. At the top end the three-storey building was the Butcher's Arms, later to become Whitaker's dyeworks.

Lower Collin Croft
pen, conté and watercolour 1950
27 x 22

This drawing shows the lower part of Collin Croft with the backs of the houses on Beast Banks above.

Collin Croft Stairs
pen, ink and watercolour
22 x 26

The buildings in the upper part of Collin Croft had been used for a variety of trades – an earthenware and pottery warehouse, a printing works and a tobacco factory. Another building housed a stable and a brass foundry.
As one of the best surviving parts of the town Kendal Civic Society had in 1975 been responsible for repairing the cobbled paving and stone steps leading up Beast Banks.
When the property at the west end of the Croft came up for sale in 1977 the Society formed a Buildings Preservation Trust to save the buildings from demolition and to convert them into dwellings. The work was completed in 1980 and won a Civic Trust Award.

Washing
pen, ink and watercolour 1957
31 x 24

An intriguing view through a doorway near the top of Collin Croft showing steps leading to the back doors of some of the houses on Beast Banks.

Collin Croft looking back
pen, ink and watercolour 1950
30 x 23

The view looking down the steps from Beast Banks.

Monument House
pen, ink and watercolour 1951
29 x 39

This house, near the top of Beast Banks, was originally a Presbyterian Chapel. It was purchased by Edward Burton about 1860. He added the verandah and two false wings and built a coach house at one corner of the frontage and a summerhouse at the other. Since this drawing was made the house has been converted into flats and a bungalow built in the garden behind the large beech tree.
The monument referred to stands on the motte of Castle Howe to the rear of the house. It is an obelisk erected in 1788 to commemorate the 'Glorious Revolution' of 1688.

Cliff Terrace
pen, ink, watercolour and chalk 1958
24 x 32

This informal terrace of houses, high above the town, was built between 1851 and 1853.

Chapel View, the large villa at the far end, was added in 1866.

Sepulchre Lane from Serpentine Road
watercolour 1954
35 x 29

Sepulchre Lane takes its name from a Quaker burial ground near the lower end. The lane rises steeply and then more gradually to meet Serpentine Road at the top of Fellside.
The houses on the right face on to Serpentine Road. Those on the left have been demolished and replaced.

Rosemary Lane
pen and wash 1960
31 x 24

Much of Fellside including Rosemary Lane (left of foreground) has been rebuilt but the houses seen here at the top of the steps still exist.

Grandy Nook
watercolour 1977
29 x 39

Grandy Nook is the name of the group of houses on the right of this watercolour which shows the view looking south along Low Fellside. On the gable wall of this building is a stone tablet with the initials of Thomas and Katherine Sandes and the date 1659. On the front is an oak panel with the date 1669.

The building was restored in 1864 and again in 1964.

Low Fellside
watercolour 1977
26 x 37

An early morning view looking north. The apparently single storey building in the centre is the upper part of the three storey former Whitaker's dyeworks at the head of the Old Shambles.

Jordan's Granary
pen and wash 1968
17 x 31

The building on the right with the ventilation turret was the warehouse of J. Jordan & Sons, corn merchants, which stood at the head of Allhallows Lane at its junction with Beast Banks and Low Fellside.

The granary and the cottages on the left were demolished in 1971 to widen the access to Low Fellside.

4 STRAMONGATE

Stramongate leads from the town centre and over the river to the north and east. This chapter includes Kent Street and several yards between Stramongate and the New Road,

Above is a page from a sketchbook showing two ideas for a painting of the New Road looking towards Lowther Street. There was at that time a telephone kiosk at the corner of Kent Street and a market stall on Saturdays.

Painters at Work
pencil 1952
55 x 37

The drawing shows Braithwaite's baker's shop and café, run for many years by Mrs Dodd, at the corner of Stramongate and Branthwaite Brow. The view continues down Kent Street to the chimney at Castle Mills.

Kent Street
pen, ink and watercolour 1950
24 x 31

No. 10, the building colourwashed red, was the office of M.B. Hodgson and the Kendal Auction Mart, who had it demolished and rebuilt in 1964. It had formerly been a warehouse for the Kendal Co-operative Society.

The adjoining British Legion Ivy Leaf Club has been altered since the date of this drawing.

Warehouse in Kent Street
conté drawing 1952
30 x 24

On the opposite (west) side of the street was a boot and shoe warehouse, now drastically extended and operated as licensed premises.

The Back of Stramongate
pen, ink and watercolour 1964
31 x 24

This view of the rear of Nos. 1 and 3 Stramongate is enlivened by washing hanging out in the yard at the back of the Kent Tavern.

Yard 11 Stramongate
pen, ink and watercolour 1952
24 x 31

At the right hand side of this drawing is the rear wing of No. 7 Stramongate, originally the town house of the Bellingham family. It became a shop in the nineteenth century and is now Henry Roberts' bookshop.

The yard was formerly known as Badenock's Yard after a Scottish gardener who lived here following his retirement from Levens Hall.
Across the end of the yard was Bill Park's picture framing workshop. The arched entry and the buildings on the extreme left have been demolished and replaced.

Yard 15 Stramongate
pen, ink, watercolour and chalk 1952
three drawings each 30 x 24

This yard was swept away and now forms a car park for the residents of Beacon Court.

Note the handcarts, a common form of transport used by tradesmen fifty years ago.

A Builder's Yard at the rear of No. 25 Stramongate
pen, ink and watercolour 1951
24 x 31

The builder's yard opened onto New Road. On the right is the Catholic Church.

Demolition
pen, ink and watercolour 1966
25 x 39

Webb's Commercial Hotel being demolished to make way for Blackhall Road.

Threlfall's Café (St George's Cocoa Rooms) was demolished at the same time.

5 ALONG THE RIVER

As in many towns the river was the life-blood of Kendal industries, providing water for washing and other purposes but above all the main source of power before the canal was constructed to bring coal to the town.

Miller Bridge
pen and ink
28 x 38

Stramongate Bridge
watercolour 1973
27 x 38

Stramongate Bridge is one of two medieval bridges in Kendal. Although it was widened in 1794 the original structure can still be seen between the more recent facings.

The building shown here abutting the north east corner of the bridge was a tannery for many years and then became a warehouse for C. & M. Pickles, fellmongers and woollen merchants. It was partly demolished and extended to become the Riverside Hotel.

Dusk over the River
watercolour 1951
23 x 38

The tranquil evening view from a point east of the bridge shows the still waters above the weir with Gooseholme in the middle. The telegraph poles march into the distance which is punctuated by the chimneys of Gilbert Gilkes & Gordon and of Goodacre's.

Until the flood relief works in the 1970s the weir crossed the river diagonally directing water in a head race below Thorny Hills to feed Castle Mills.

Below Stramongate Weir
watercolour 1950
22 x 28

The pink-washed building was originally another tannery.

Reflections
watercolour 1950
23 x 31

Here the pink-washed buildings are reflected in the still waters of the mill-dam. Behind is the Sand Aire Chapel, beyond which can be seen the roof of the Provincial building before its enlargement in the late 1950s.

The building on the right adjoined the Bridge Inn. It had originally been a mill but became a house in the nineteenth century.

Kendal Fair from Little Aynam
ink, watercolour and chalk 1957
23 x 51

The fair on New Road is seen reflected in the mill race, the river running at a lower level between. An overflow weir separated the mill race from the river. The footbridge and Gooseholme appear on the right. The mill race has now been filled in and here forms part of a putting green.

Early Morning Reflections
pen, ink and watercolour 1951
23 x 29

The mill race heads towards Castle Mills. A three arched bridge carries Bridge Street over it. The foreground is now a car park.

There have been mills on this site since the thirteenth century and they have served a variety of the town's industries. In 1806 they were rebuilt by William Braithwaite and Isaac Wilson and later this firm became J.J. and W. Wilson, manufacturers of travelling rugs, tweed and horse collar checks. From 1933 Goodacre & Co. made carpets here.

Aynam Lodge
watercolour 1978
36 x 54

The rather imposing house facing the river next to Miller Bridge was built for Thomas Harrison, surgeon, in 1825. It was designed by the Websters.

This drawing shows the house before renovation by Gilbert Gilkes & Gordon.

Aynam Lodge
pen, ink and watercolour 1950
30 x 23

Here we see the rear of Aynam Lodge facing Bridge Lane opposite the mason's yard. The surgeon's consulting room was in the far wing approached by a verandah.

The Mason's Yard
pen, ink and watercolour 1950
28 x 38
(private collection)

The yard and office of J. W. Howie & Sons, well known builders in Kendal, lay between Bridge Lane and the mill race. This also is now a car park.

Miller Bridge
watercolour 1999
48 x 38
(private collection)

Miller Bridge was built in 1818 to replace an earlier structure and to facilitate access to the warehouses at Canal Head. The canal, completed in 1819, brought coal into Kendal from Lancashire and carried out limestone and manufactured goods. As a result, coal replaced water power with steam power, enabling Kendal's manufacturing industry to expand.

The bridge was designed by the Kendal architect Francis Webster who also designed the buildings seen beyond the bridge which were offices and showrooms for his marble-polishing mill.

Waterside
pastel
27 x 32

An evening view showing the west bank of the river below Miller Bridge with the houses of Gawith Place against the background of trees above Garth Heads.

Nether Bridge
pencil drawing 1981
18 x 23

Nether Bridge was constructed to carry the main road to Lancaster and the south over the river. In 1376 Edward III granted a right of pontage to charge tolls for repair.

The original bridge was very narrow: it was widened on the north side in 1772 and again in 1908.

6 KIRKLAND

The first Norman Baron of Kendal, Ivo de Tailebois, gave the church of Kendal with its land – Kirkland – to the Abbey of St. Mary at York. Until 1908 Kirkland was a township separate from Kendal.

Kendal Parish Church
Pencil drawing
A church is recorded in the Domesday Book of 1086 but the earliest parts of the present building are thirteenth century; most of the fabric dates from between 1400-1600.

The Old Grammar School
watercolour 1984
27 x 36

A Chantry School was founded in 1525 but the present building was erected in 1588 after the school had been re-founded as a Grammar School following the Reformation. It moved to new premises in 1889.

Part of this building is now the education department of Abbot Hall Art Gallery and the other half is a private house.

Abbot Hall Stables
watercolour 1969
28 x 37
(private collection)

In medieval times a house was built to the north of the church for the Abbot of St Mary's, York when visiting the abbey lands. The present house was built in 1759 for Col. George Wilson to the design of John Carr of York. After many changes of ownership and a period of neglect it was converted to an Art Gallery in 1962.

The stables are said to be built on the site of the Abbot's house. This view shows the stable yard with its archway leading to the forecourt of the house. To the right is the back of the old Grammar School and beyond is the tower of the Parish Church. The painting was made shortly before work commenced on the conversion of the stables into the Museum of Lakeland Life and Industry.

Kirkbarrow Lane
pencil 1975
35 x 24

Kirkbarrow Lane is a narrow passageway leading from the west side of Kirkland to Kirkbarrow House, once the home of Cornelius Nicholson, the nineteenth century historian of Kendal.

Blindbeck
watercolour and chalk 1985
34 x 26

Blindbeck is probably so called because the source of the stream is hidden in the rock fissures of Kendal Fell. It was formerly the boundary between the borough of Kendal and the township of Kirkland.

Blindbeck runs between the two buildings shown here and under the road in the foreground.
On the right is the back of Blindbeck House, built in 1785 by Christopher Wilson, hosier and banker.
In the 1950s it was the Queen's Hotel and is now converted into apartments.

7 FROM MY WINDOW

For most of my life I have been fortunate to work in a first floor 'Room with a View'. Here are some of the sketches and paintings I have been able to make.

Above is the last of a fleet of horse drawn delivery lorries used by the railway. I believe the driver's name was Edwin. Such was the lock on the front axle of his vehicle that he was able to perform a u-turn in Lowther Street.

Across the River
watercolour 1978
53 x 37

This view shows Miller Bridge with Aynam Lodge on the left. To the right Bridge Street leads to Canal Head and the Castle stands at the top of the hill beyond.

The coming of the railway led to a decline in canal traffic and in 1856 the warehouses became an engineering works, since considerably enlarged by Gilbert Gilkes & Gordon.

Kendal Fair
watercolour 1952
29 x 23
(private collection)

Hiring fairs for agricultural labourers and domestic servants were held in Kendal at Whitsuntide and Martinmas. The accompanying entertainments have survived to this day. Here we see a roundabout being erected on a typically wet day.

Early Morning Mist
watercolour 1979
24 x 29

Mist rising from the river partially obscures the buildings beyond, including the gasometer.

Gulfs Road
watercolour 1982
36 x 32

Gulfs Road takes its name from The Gulfs which were a series of narrow passages connecting one yard to the next, providing an escape route from flooding along the lower ends of the yards. The road was built to provide easier access to Braithwaite's mill and other commercial premises.

In the centre is the yard owned by N. Greenbank & Co., scrap metal merchants and car dismantlers. Just beyond is the newly built Old People's Welfare centre.
Dowkers Lane now cuts across between this and the buildings on Highgate. Edgecombe Court and a car park replace the scrap yard.

Gawith Place
watercolour 1980
25 x 30

Shown here are the then recently renovated houses of Gawith Place, beyond which the construction of the south east Highgate housing continues.

Kendal Roofscape
watercolour 1997
53 x 45

Not from my window but from the scaffolding erected when the roof was reslated. This view shows the Town Hall on the opposite side of Lowther Street. On the skyline to the left are the houses on Cliff Terrace and Serpentine Road.

The Town Hall was originally the White Hall Assembly Rooms, built in 1825. In 1859 Kendal Corporation converted the premises into a town hall to replace the Moot Hall at the corner of the Market Place. It was extensively redesigned and enlarged in 1893-7 when the present tower was built.

Extract from 1853 map of Kendal
Locations marked by page numbers

66
67
69
68
70
71
72
73
74
62
St George's Church
BADGER CLOSE
Common Garden
Castle Barn
Goose Holme
Sand Area
Duke Charles Inn
Friends' Meeting Ho.
Roman Cath. Chapel
Ireland's Manufactory
KENT TERRACE
THOS FELL
G. UNTHANK
J. J. WILSON
E. W. SCOTT
GEO. GIBSON
Miss Rooking
Geo. Webster
GEO. HINDE
G. WEBSTER
CORPORATION
Wiggy Bottom
GREAT
AYNAM
Aynam Lodge
CANAL HEAD
Coal Yards
COAL WHARVES
Canal Basin
COAL WHARVES
WAREHOUSES
Marble Works
Castle Mills
Common Garden
or
NURSERY GROUND
Castle Lodge
WILLIAM THOMPSON
NEW ROAD

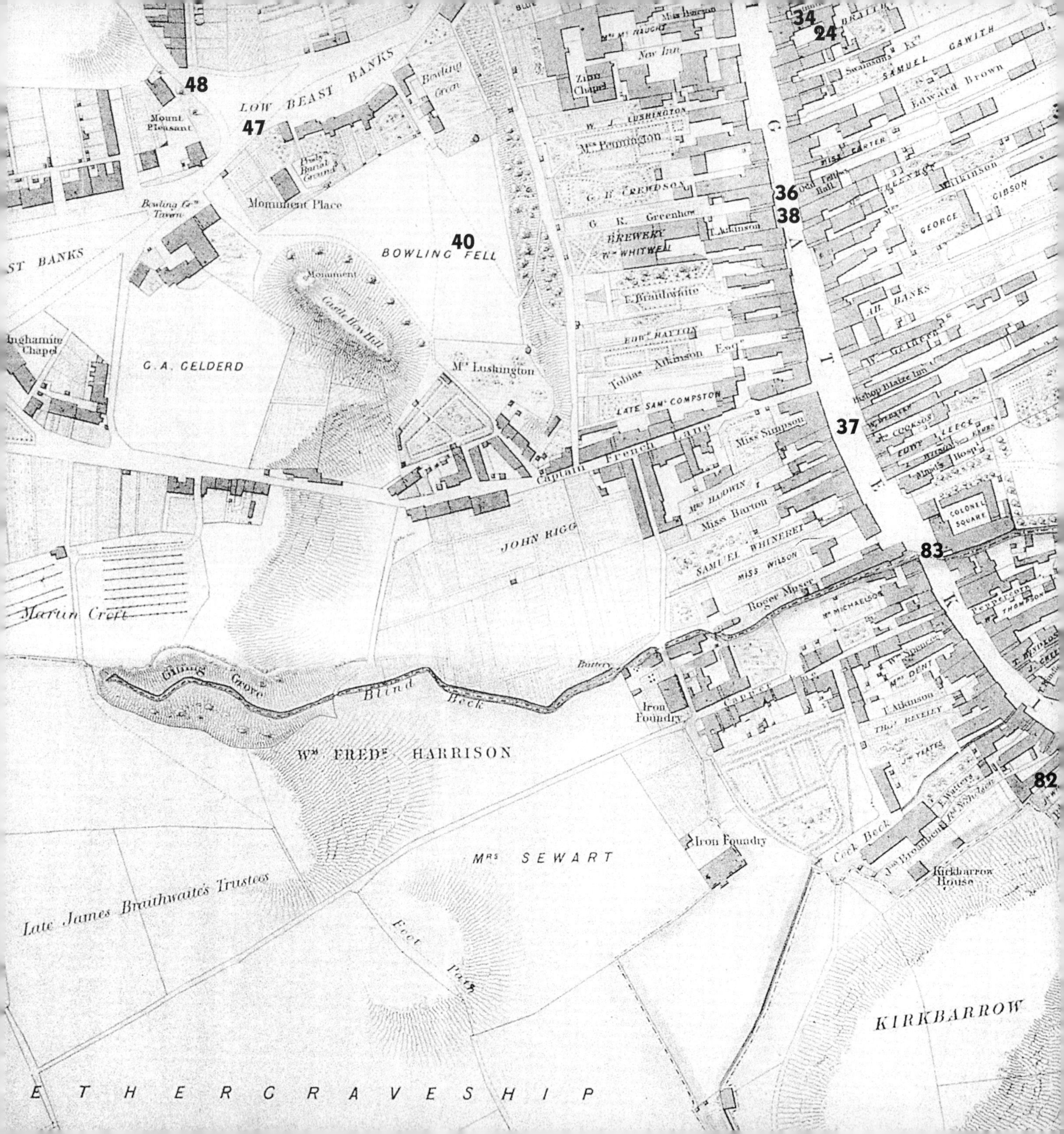

34
24
48
LOW BEAST BANKS
Mount Pleasant
47
Bowling Green
Zion Chapel
New Inn
SAMUEL GAWITH
Edward Brown
W. J. LUSHINGTON
Mrs Pennington
MISS CARTER
Friends Burial Ground
Monument Place
Bowling Gn. Tavern
G. B. CREWDSON
36
38
Odd Fellows Hall
Wilkinson
GIBSON
G. R. Greenhow
T. Atkinson
BREWERY
Wm. WHITWELL
GEORGE
40
BOWLING FELL
ST BANKS
Monument
Castle How Hill
T. Braithwaite
AB. BANKS
Inghamite Chapel
G. A. GELDERD
Mr. Lushington
EDWd. RATTON
Tobias Atkinson Esqre.
Bishop Blaize Inn
LATE SAML. COMPSTON
Miss Simpson
37
Captain French Lane
COOKSON
Mrs. HODWIN
Miss Barton
COLONEL SQUARE
JOHN RIGG
SAMUEL WHINERET
83
MISS WILSON
Martin Croft
Roger Moser
Mrs. MICHAELSON
THOMPSON
Battery
Gilling Grove
Blind Beck
Wm. Spencer
Mrs. DENT
Iron Foundry
T. Atkinson
THOs. REVELEY
Wm. FREDK. HARRISON
Jn. YEATES
82
Iron Foundry
Cock Beck
Mrs. SEWART
Kirkbarrow House
Late James Braithwaite's Trustees
Foot Path
KIRKBARROW
N E T H E R G R A V E S H I P

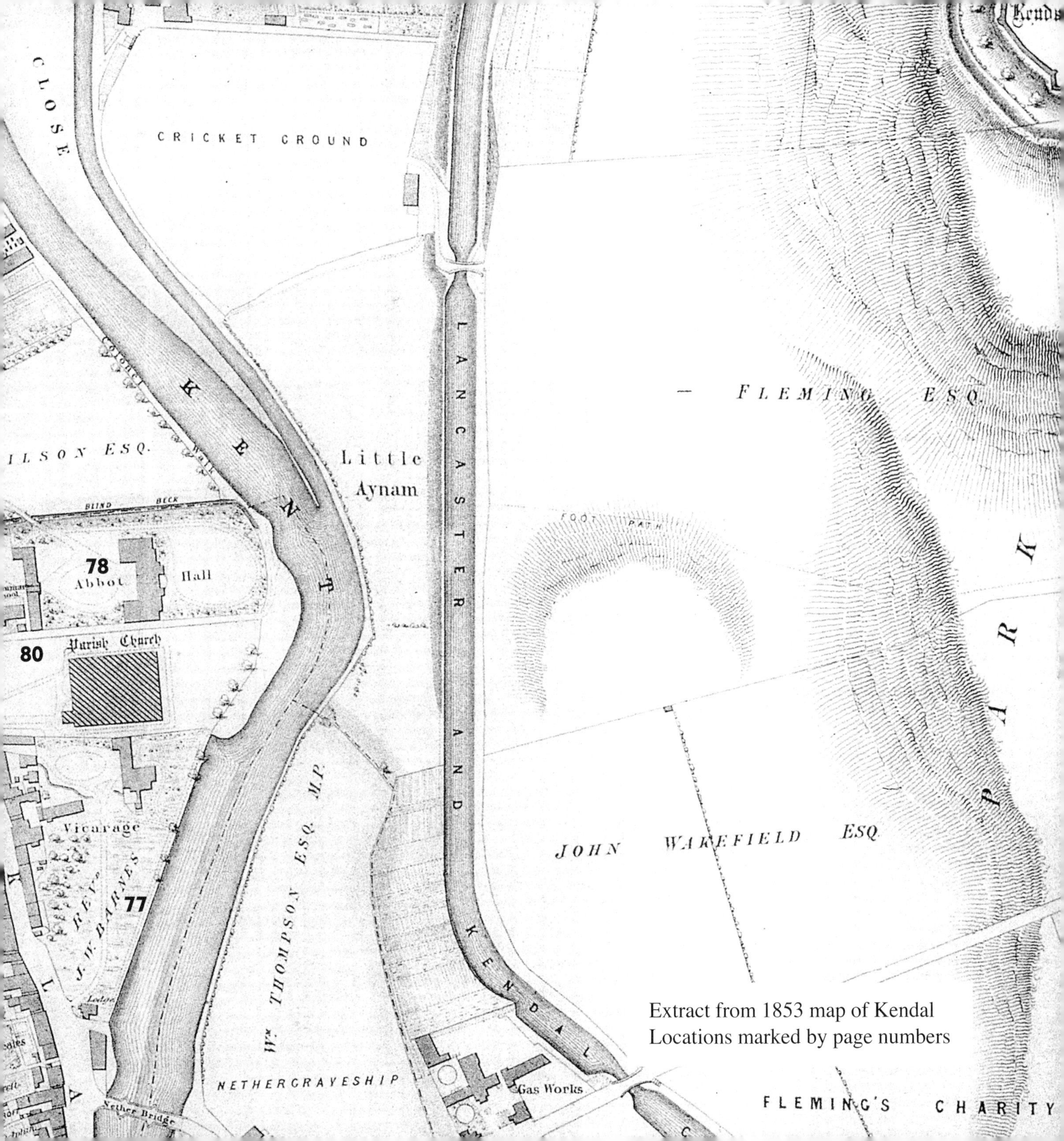

Extract from 1853 map of Kendal
Locations marked by page numbers

A Bus Queue in Highgate
pastel
31 x 16

The end of the day – and of this book.

QUILT IT AS YOU GO

5 different ways to quilt as you piece

Edited by Carolyn S. Vagts

Annie's®

Introduction

Not all quilters are skilled in the actual quilting process. Many enjoy the piecing and are mystified as to how to finish their quilt. Sometimes it boils down to economics.

For many quilters it's hard to piece a quilt top, and then hand it off to someone else to finish. This book gives quilters alternatives to finishing quilts. There are several ways to accomplish what is referred to as "quilt as you go" technique.

Here you will find 10 projects that can all be quilted at the same time that you are piecing them. For many of these techniques, increasing size is a matter of continuing on with extra blocks and rows. You decide just how big or small you want to go. The process is the same for all sizes. Once you learn these fun techniques you'll discover all the possibilities and the freedom that opens up for you.

There's everything from baby quilts and table toppers to runners and bed-size quilts. Most of these projects could easily be adjusted to different sizes simply by adding more sections or rows. These are techniques you can adapt to other projects. Learn to quilt a bargello quilt as it is pieced, or create scrappy blocks ahead of time and work on them when you need a portable project. These techniques will quickly become some of your favorites.

If you're looking for options for quilting, look no further.

Table of Contents

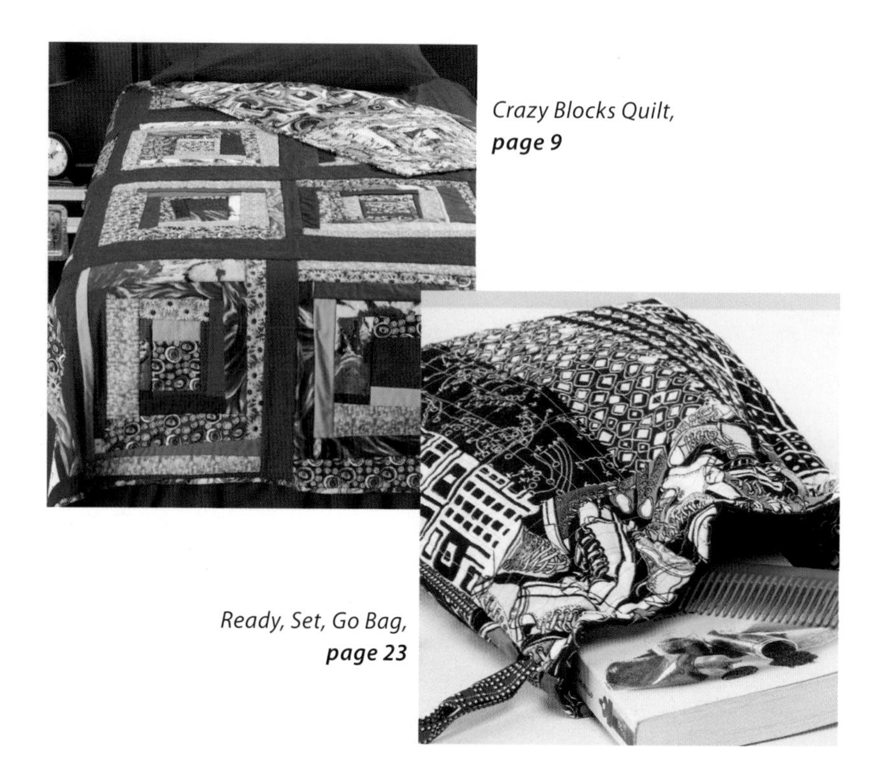

Crazy Blocks Quilt, ***page 9***

Ready, Set, Go Bag, ***page 23***

Code of Love Bed Runner

Designed and Quilted by Gina Gempesaw

Use the Morse code chart to create your own secret message or to decode the one in this modern graphic bed runner.

Specifications

Skill Level: Confident Beginner
Bed Runner Size: 50¼" x 18"

Materials

- ⅝ yard red tonal
- 1¾ yards white tonal
- Low-loft cotton batting 22" x 54"
- 1¾ yards backing
- Thread
- Fabric basting spray
- Basic sewing tools and supplies

Cutting

From red tonal:

- Cut 2 (2½" by fabric width) A strips.
- Cut 4 (2¼" by fabric width) binding strips.

From white tonal:

- Cut 1 each:
  7½" by fabric width B strip
  9½" by fabric width C strip
  7" by fabric width D strip
  10" by fabric width E strip
- Cut 1 (18½" by fabric width) strip.
  Subcut into 13 (1¾" x 18½") F strips.

From backing:
- Cut 1 (23" x 55") rectangle along the lengthwise grain.

Assembly

1. Stitch one each A, B and C strips together to create a strip set referring to Figure 1; press seams toward A.

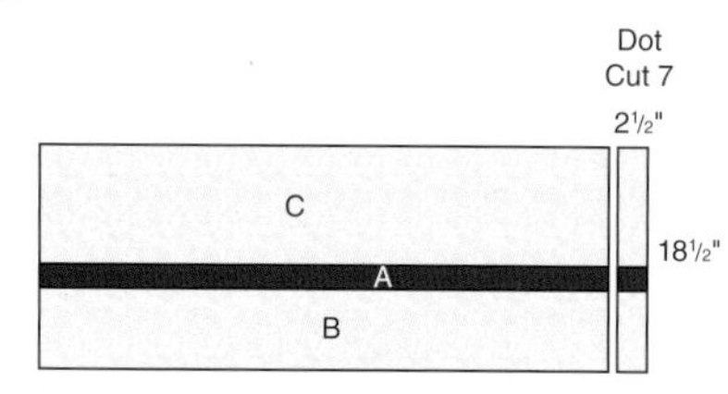

Figure 1

2. Cut the C-A-B strip set into seven 2½" x 18½" Dot units referring again to Figure 1.

3. Stitch one each A, D and E strips together to create a strip set referring to Figure 2; press seams toward A.

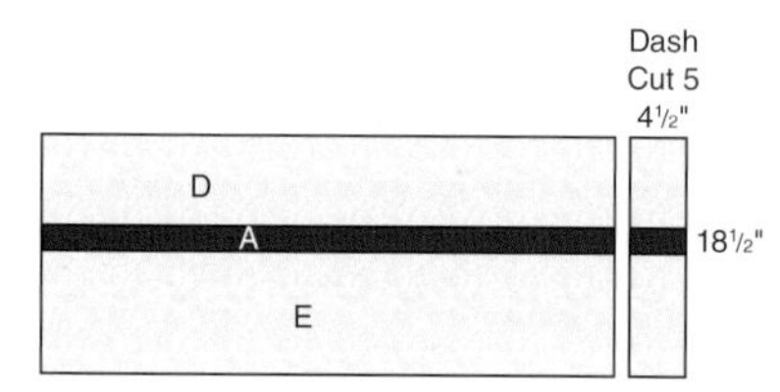

Figure 2

4. Cut the D-A-E strip set into five 4½" x 18½" Dash units referring again to Figure 2.

5. Arrange Dot and Dash units in order to spell the word "love" referring to Figure 3. Insert F strips between the units.

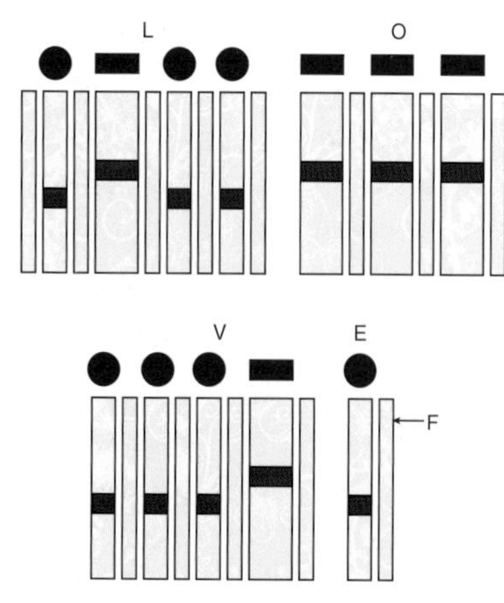

Figure 3

6. Follow manufacturer's instructions to layer and spray-baste batting to wrong side of backing.

7. For stitching guidelines, mark a line 1½" away from one long edge of batting/backing unit. Mark a second line 18½" away from the first as shown in Figure 4. Mark a third line 1½" away from one short side of unit.

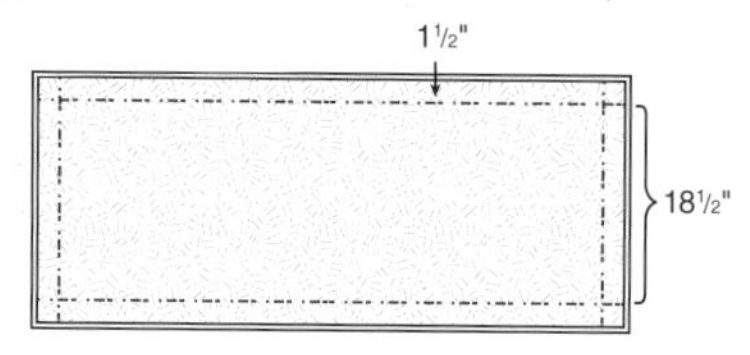

Figure 4

8. Working from left to right, position the first F strip right side up, matching one long edge to the vertical stitching guideline and short ends to the top and bottom horizontal stitching guidelines. Baste to hold ⅛" from the left-hand long edge (Figure 5).

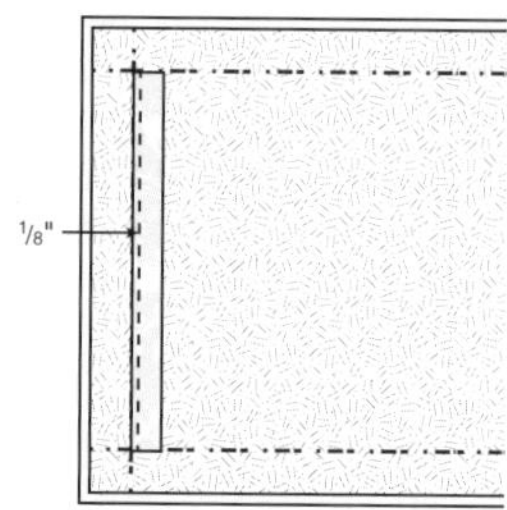

Figure 5

9. Position and pin a Dot unit, right sides together, on the right-hand long edge of the F strip (Figure 6a). Stitch ¼" seam allowance, press Dot unit away from F (Figure 6b).

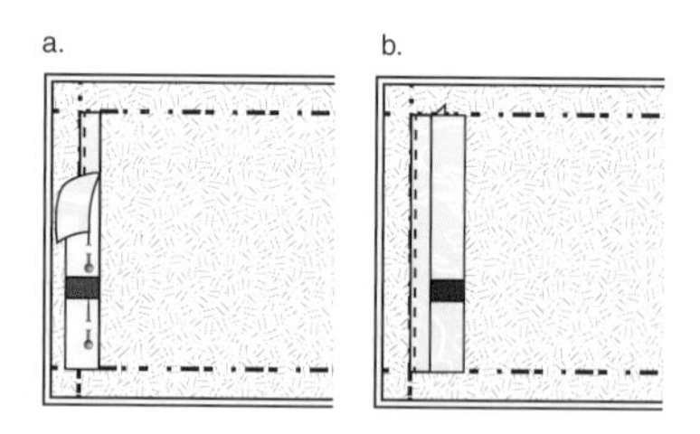

Figure 6

Gina Suggests

In this project, pressing after stitching each seam helps to set the seam and makes for a smooth quilt.

10. Continue adding F strips, and Dot and Dash units as arranged using the stitch-and-flip technique.

Gina Suggests

Add extra quilting to each strip before adding the next one. Plan your quilting so that there will be no need to match up quilting lines from strip to strip.

For example: Stitch horizontal lines in one strip and vertical lines in the next, and skip quilting the F strips. Or quilt only the background area leaving the dots and dashes un-quilted to make them "pop" out of the quilt background.

11. Baste ⅛" from pieced table runner outer edges. Trim batting and backing to match pieced top. Bind using the 2¼" strips to complete the bed runner. ■

"The simplicity of the dots and dashes in the Morse code reminds me of minimalist modern quilts. A quilt could hold a secret message—literally!"
—Gina Gempesaw

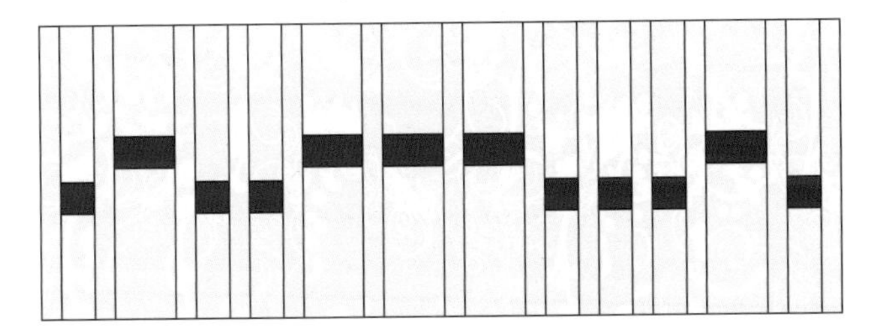

Code of Love Bed Runner
Placement Diagram 50¼" x 18"

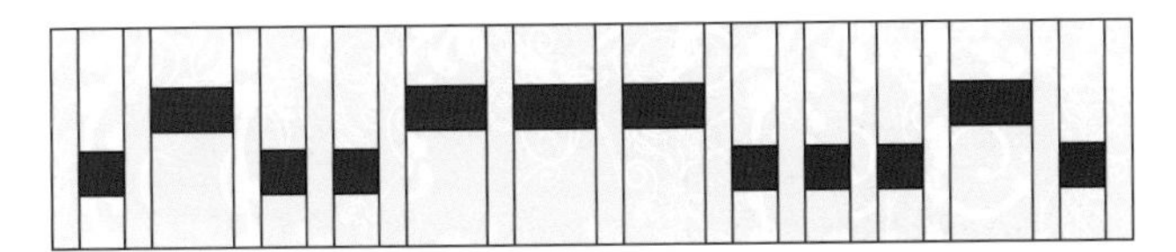

Code of Love Bed Runner Alternate Size
Placement Diagram 50¼" x 10"
Note: *Reduce white tonal to 1 yard and cut B 3½" wide, C 5½" wide, D 3" wide, E 6" wide and F 10½" wide, all by fabric width strips referring to cutting instructions. All other cutting and assembly instructions are the same for this narrower size.*

Morse Code Messages

The dots and dashes used to indicate letters in Morse code are perfect for making a very graphic two-color quilt with a hidden message. Include a key for the letters with the quilt or on the quilt label so that the recipient can decipher the message.

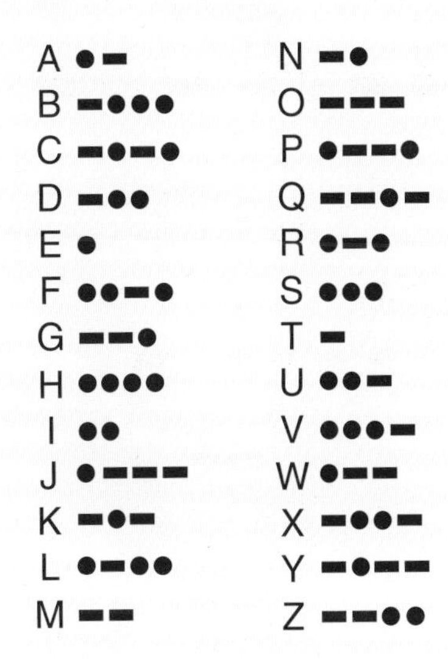

Figure A

Quilt-As-You-Go String Pieced Blocks

These blocks are a great project when time is at a premium but you want to have something to work on. Keep a box of scrap strips and precut squares of batting and backing fabric ready to stitch when the opportunity arises.

This technique works the same on all sizes and is a great way to use the scraps of batting and fabric lying around your sewing room.

Completing the Blocks

1. Cut a fabric backing and batting piece at least ½"–1" larger than the unfinished block size you want to make. For example, if making a 9½" x 9½" unfinished block, cut 10"–11" squares. ***Note:*** *Cutting these pieces larger than the desired block size allows for quilting shrinkage. You will square up the completed blocks to make connecting the blocks easier.*

2. Position the batting on the wrong side of the backing fabric, matching the raw edges.

3. Select two strips of fabric any width but long enough to extend past the diagonal of the batting and backing fabric. With right sides together, pin the two strips in place diagonally across the batting/backing piece. Stitch a ¼" seam through all layers (Photo 1).

Photo 1

4. Press strips open. Add a third strip to the second strip following step 3. Press strips open and repeat (Photo 2).

Photo 2

5. Continue adding strips to both sides of the first strip. Pressing after each strip is stitched down until you have covered the entire batting/backing piece (Photo 3).

Photo 3

6. Square up the block from the backing side of the quilted piece to complete a quilt-as-you-go block (Photo 4).

Photo 4

Joining the Blocks

To connect the blocks you will need a fabric, easily found, like black, if you will be making this over a period of time. The amount needed depends on how big you will be making your quilt. It is better to have too much than too little.

1. Trim all blocks to a consistent size.

2. Cut two different width strips for the connecting channels; 1⅛"- and 1⅝"-wide strips by the fabric width.

3. Fold and press the 1⅝" channel strip in half lengthwise wrong sides together and cut length to match block size (Photo 5).

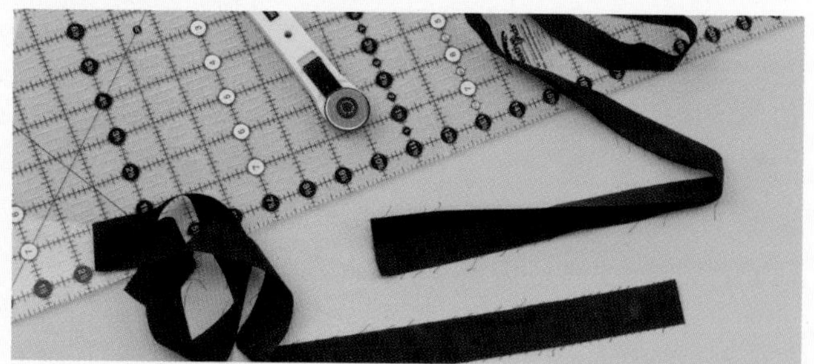

Photo 5

4. Position and pin the folded strip along one edge of the back of a trimmed block with raw edges aligned (Photo 6).

Photo 6

5. Position and pin a 1⅛" channel strip right sides together on the front side of the block (Photo 7).

Photo 7

6. Stitch along the edge through all layers using a ¼" seam. Trim channel strips flush with the block edges.

7. Press the 1⅛" channel strip toward the raw edges, extending over the block edge. Turn the block wrong side up and slip a second block right side up under the unit. Align the second block with the opposite edge of the 1⅛" strip. Stitch in place. (Photo 8). ***Note:*** *Both right sides of the two blocks should be on the same side with a connecting channel strip in between.*

Photo 8

8. Flip the block unit over so that both backing fabrics are showing. Press the double-folded channel over and pin. Use a slipstitch to sew in place to complete a two-block unit (Photo 9).

Photo 9

9. Repeat steps 2–8 to make two two-block units.

10. To connect the two-block units, repeat the same process of adding the folded channel strip to the back of the units and the 1⅛" strip to the front. Flip to the back and slipstitch in place to complete a four-block unit (Photo 10).

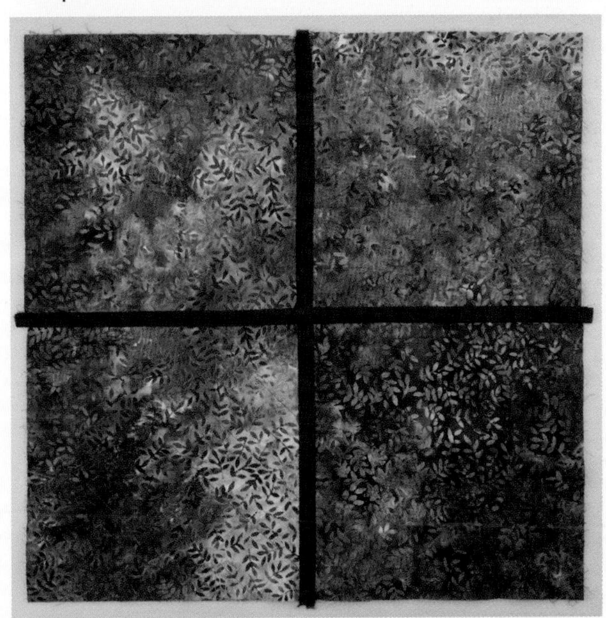

Photo 10

11. Continue to make four-block units until you have the number of blocks required for your quilt. Connect the four-block units using the same channeling technique. ***Note:*** *You can also attach in rows using the same technique if you prefer.* ■

Crazy Blocks Quilt

Designed and Quilted by Carol Zentgraf

This quilt uses the quilt-as-you-go method with strips of all different sizes and shapes, so no two blocks are the same. Some of the strips are leftovers from other projects and are already pieced together, creating a truly scrappy quilt.

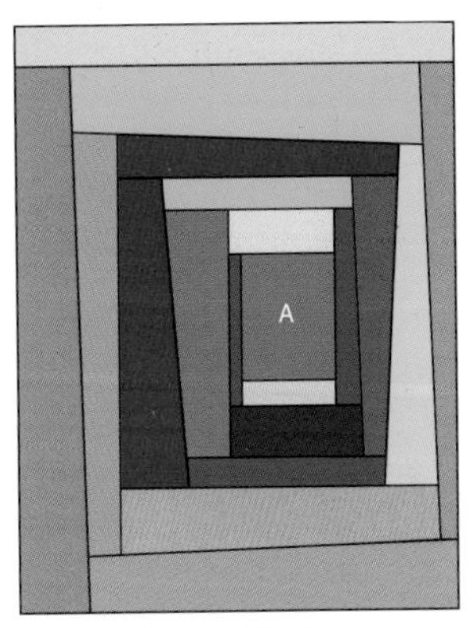

Crazy Blocks
14"–15" x 16"–18"
Make 16

Specifications

Skill Level: Advanced
Quilt Size: 64" x 80"
Block Size: Approximately 14"–15" x 16"–18"
Number of Blocks: 16

Materials

- Assorted print and solid fabrics to total 10 yards for blocks, sashing and binding
- 3 yards 90"-wide cotton batting
- Thread
- Fusible web tape
- Basic sewing tools and supplies

Cutting

From assorted prints & solids:

- Cut 32 (4" x 4") A squares.
  16 of the squares are for the block back center.
- Cut 3"–5"-wide strips for B and C sashing strips.
- Cut and piece 2¼"-wide strips for binding to total 290".
- Cut all remaining fabrics for front and back blocks into 1½"–3½"-wide strips.

From batting:

- Cut batting strips to match the width sizes of each block strip.
- Cut 16 (4") batting squares.

Completing the Blocks

Refer to Log Cabin Quilt As You Go for specifics of this technique.

1. Layer the backing A square right side down, batting and front-side A square right side up; pin to hold. ***Note:*** *Layers of three pieces (backing, batting and front) are referred to as a set in the instructions that follow.*

2. To add the first set of strips to the center A set, select one same-size front strip, back strip and batting strip a little longer than one side of the center square. ***Note:*** *It isn't necessary to measure the length of the strips as long as they are slightly longer than the edge you will be sewing them to.*

3. Place the front-side strip along one edge of the front side of the A set with right sides together. Place the backing strip along the same edge of the back of the A set.

4. Place the batting strip on the top side of the front-side strip. Stitch the layers together using a ¼" seam allowance as shown in Figure 1. Trim the batting close to the stitching referring to Figure 2.

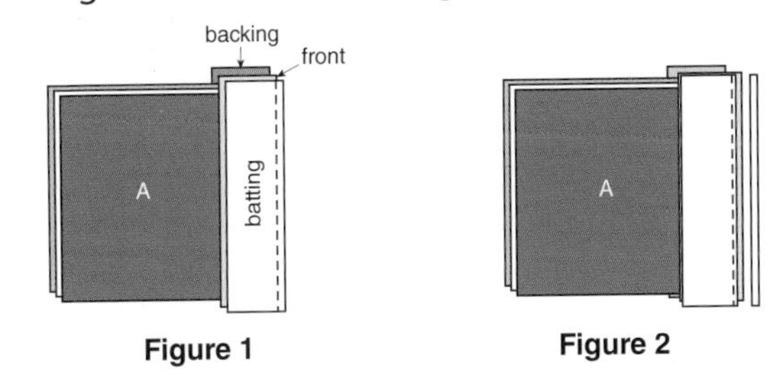

Figure 1 **Figure 2**

Here's a Tip

If you find stitching ¼" seams with all the layers to be difficult, try using a ½" seam allowance and trim to ¼" after stitching.

Log Cabin Quilt As You Go

The basic quilt-as-you-go technique refers to a stitch-and-flip process where strips are stitched to a batting-topped backing square or to the assembly of completed blocks into a quilt. A variation of this is used to create reversible blocks that feature Log Cabin piecing on both the block front and back.

Identical strips are cut for the block fabric, batting and backing fabrics and all three strips are added simultaneously. It is ideal for traditional Log Cabin piecing with straight strips or for creating an unstructured block as shown in the Crazy Blocks Quilt using the following instructions.

1. Select a mixture of five to 10 print and solid fabrics for the quilt top. ***Note:*** *You can use the same fabric for the backing strips or a variety of fabrics as for the top. The yardage needed will depend on the size of your quilt. Use needled cotton batting or other low-loft batting.*

2. From each fabric, cut a variety of strips across the width of the fabric in widths ranging from 1"–3". Repeat to cut batting strips in the same widths.

3. To begin, cut an identical center square or rectangle each from the top fabric, batting and backing. Layer the backing fabric right side down, batting and top fabric right side up.

4. To add the first set of strips to the center, select a strip width and cut one strip each from a top fabric strip, batting strip and backing fabric strip a little longer than one side of the center square. ***Note:*** *It isn't necessary to measure the length of the strips as long as they are slightly longer than the edge you will be sewing them to.*

5. Place the top strip along one edge of the center square top fabric with right sides together. Repeat to place the backing strip along the same edge of the backing fabric.

6. Place the batting strip on the wrong side of the top strip. Stitch the layers together using a ¼" seam allowance. Trim the batting close to the stitching (Photo 1).

Photo 1

7. Open the strips right sides out and press the seam allowance away from the center (Photo 2). Trim the short ends even with the center; trim the long edges even, if necessary.

Photo 2

8. Repeat step 4 to cut a set of strips slightly longer than one combined edge of the center block and first set of strips.

9. Sandwich the edge between the top and backing strips with right sides together and the batting strip on the wrong side of the top strip. Stitch the edges together; trim the batting close to the stitching (Photo 3).

Photo 3

10. Press the strips away from the center and trim the ends (Photo 4).

Photo 4

11. Continue adding strips around the block, alternating widths and fabrics as desired. To create an unstructured look, cut the long edges of random strips at an angle after stitching them to the block (Photo 5).

Photo 5

12. Piece strips around the block until it is slightly larger than the desired finished size. Trim edges and square corners as needed to complete the block (Photo 6).

Photo 6

5. Open the strips right sides out and press the seam allowance away from A. Trim the short ends even with the A set as shown in Figure 3. Cut the strips at a random angle, again referring to Figure 3.

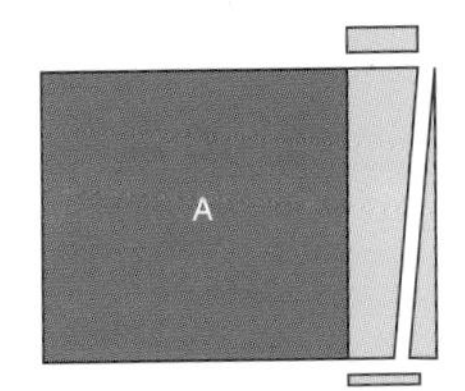

Figure 3

6. Repeat step 2 to cut a same-width set of front, backing and batting strips slightly longer than the combined edge of A and first set of added strips.

7. Sandwich the edge of the A/strip set between the front and backing strips cut in step 6 with right sides together and the batting strip on the top of the front-side strip. Stitch the edges together; trim the batting close to the stitching as in step 4.

8. Press the strips away from the center and trim the short ends even and the side at an angle as in step 5.

9. Continue adding strips around the block, alternating widths and fabrics as desired until it is 14"–15" wide and 16"–18" long. Trim edges and square corners as needed to complete one rectangle-shape Crazy block.

10. Repeat steps 1–9 to complete a total of 16 Crazy Blocks. ***Note:*** *Blocks will not all be the same size.*

Completing the Sashing

1. Select four Crazy Blocks. Measure the total width of the blocks. Subtract this measurement from 64" to determine the total B sashing strips width needed.

2. Decide how wide you want to make each of the three B sashing strips, varying the widths as desired to total the amount needed. To each B strip width, add ¾" for seam allowances.

Here's a Tip

If some blocks are shorter than others, add strips of sashing fabrics to the ends of the shorter blocks to make them all the same length as the longest block. Cut front, batting and backing strips for each set of strips as needed.

3. Sew the first set of B sashing strips to the long edge of one block in the same manner as in Completing the Blocks and as shown in Figure 4. ***Note:*** *The first seam uses a ¼" seam allowance.*

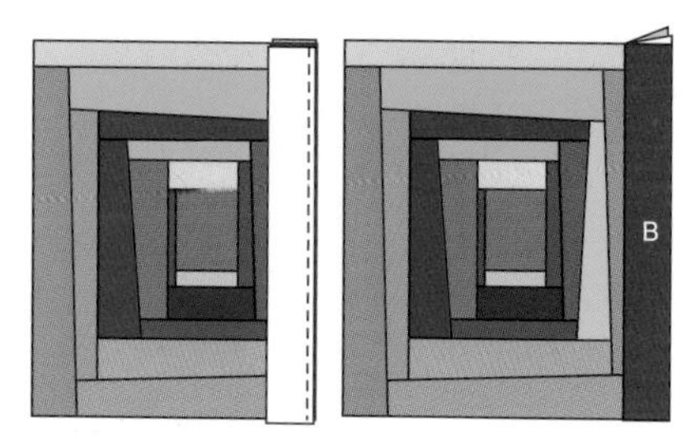

Figure 4

4. To add the next block, use a ½" seam allowance to sew the front side of the block to the right side of the front B sashing strip and batting layers only, leaving the backing strip free. Press the seam toward the B sashing strip.

5. Turn the raw edge of the backing sashing strip under ⅜" and apply fusible web tape along the edge as shown in Figure 5.

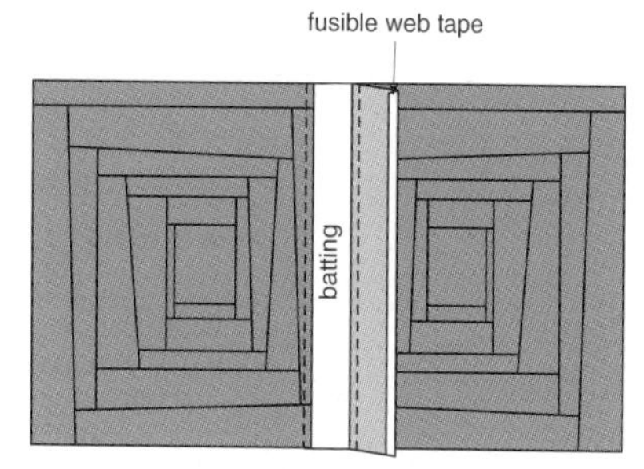

Figure 5

6. Overlap the fused edge over the ½" seam allowance on the stitched strips; fuse the edge in place.

7. From the front side, stitch in the ditch between the sashing and the block to secure the back-side sashing seam.

8. Repeat steps 3–7 to assemble the remaining selected blocks and short sashing B strips to complete one row.

9. Repeat steps 1–8 to complete a total of four block rows.

10. Measure the combined height of the block rows and subtract from 84" to determine the total finished width of the long sashing strips.

11. Prepare long sashing C strips and join rows as in steps 2–7 to complete the quilt front and backing.

Completing the Quilt

1. Join the 2¼"-wide binding strips on the short ends with diagonal seams to make a 290"-long binding strip referring to Figure 6; trim seams to ¼" and press seams open.

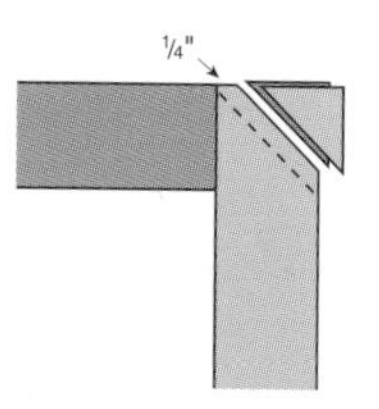

Figure 6

2. Bind quilt using 2¼" strips to complete quilt. ■

Crazy Blocks
Placement Diagram 64" x 80"

Baby A-Go-Go

Designed & Quilted by CJ Behling

Use this version of the easy stitch-and-flip technique to complete this baby quilt in a weekend. When you're done, you're done.

Specifications

Skill Level: Confident Beginner
Quilt Size: 50" x 56"

Materials

- 7/8 yard cream/white tonal
- 1 5/8 yards green dot
- 1 5/8 yards brown solid
- 1 2/3 yards multistripe
- 1 3/4 yards yellow dot
- 1 7/8 yards 96"-wide batting
- Thread
- Fabric-basting spray (optional)
- Even-feed or walking presser foot
- Basic sewing tools and supplies

Cutting

From cream/white tonal:

- Cut 1 (26" by fabric width) strip.
  Subcut 2 (20" x 26") A rectangles.

From green dot:

- Cut 9 (5" by fabric width) strips.
  Subcut 4 (5" x 35") G border strips.
  Set aside 5 strips for H borders.

From brown solid:

- Cut 9 (5" by fabric width) strips.
  Subcut 4 each 5" x 27" E and 5" x 41" F border strips from 8 strips.
  From remaining strip, subcut 8 (5") K squares.

From multistripe:

- Cut 6 (5" by fabric width) strips.
  Subcut 4 each 5" x 19" B and 5" x 25" C border strips.
- Cut 6 (2 3/4" by fabric width) binding strips.

From yellow dot:

- Cut 11 (5" by fabric width) strips.
  Subcut 1 strip into 8 (5") D squares.
  Set aside remaining strips for I/J borders.

From batting:

- Cut 1 (20" x 26") A rectangle, 8 (5") D squares and 2 each of the following strips:

5" x 19" B	5" x 25" C
5" x 27" E	5" x 41" F
5" x 35" G	5" x 49" H
5" x 43" I	5" x 57" J

Completing Appliqué

1. Fold and lightly press one A rectangle in half horizontally and vertically to mark center.

2. Refer to Raw-Edge Fusible Appliqué on page 17 to prepare, apply and stitch appliqué pieces provided on insert to the center of A. ***Note:*** *Keep the finished appliqué from becoming stiff by cutting out the center of the fusible web piece ½" inside the traced line in step 2 of Raw-Edge Fusible Appliqué referring to Figure 1 below. Carefully apply the fusible web to the wrong side of the fabric as shown here in Figure 2 and trim as instructed in step 3 of Raw-Edge Fusible Appliqué.*

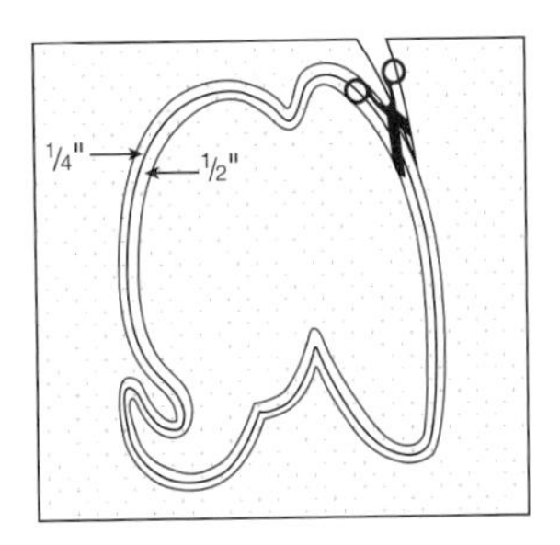

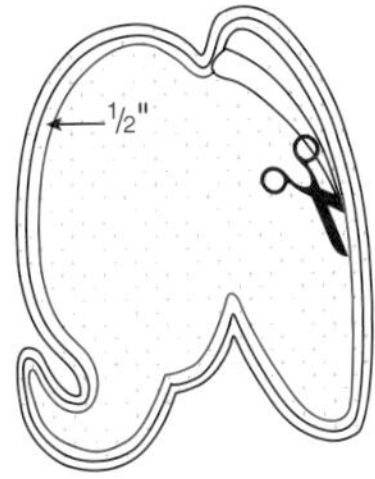

Figure 1

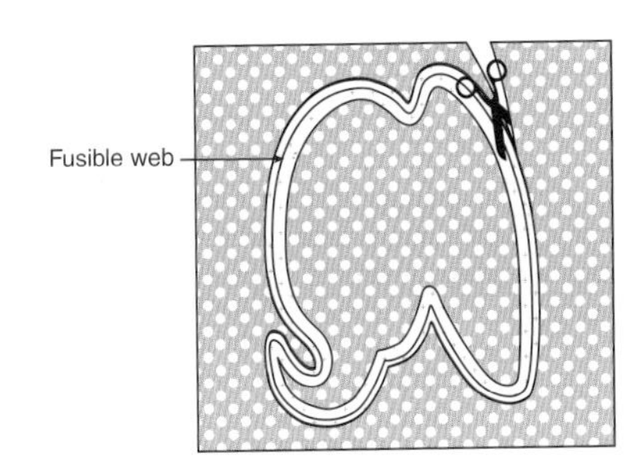

Figure 2

3. Layer second A, wrong side up, batting A and appliquéd A, right side up. Pin-, thread- or spray-baste together.

4. Follow your sewing machine manual to attach and use an even-feed or walking presser foot for the remainder of construction. This foot will feed several layers of fabric through your machine evenly, keeping layers smooth and free of puckering.

5. Quilt around the outer edge of the appliqué shapes just outside the appliqué stitching (Figure 3). Add more quilting as desired.

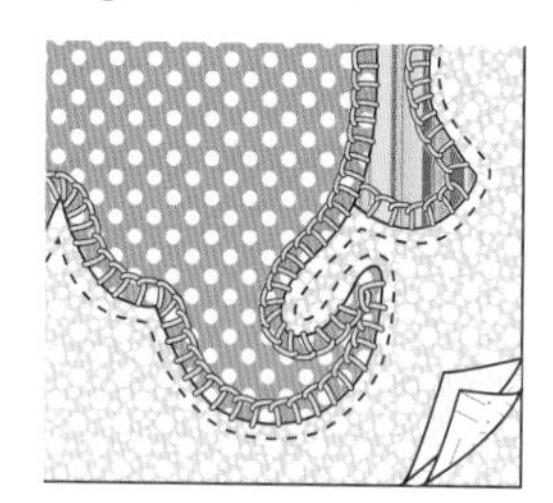

Figure 3

6. Trim quilted A to 19" x 25" to complete quilt center.

CJ Suggests

When using a low-loft polyester batting you will not need to trim the batting from the seam allowances. It adds very little bulk to the seam allowance.

If you have chosen cotton or cotton-blend low-loft batting, trim batting seam allowance only to 1⁄8" away from the seam to minimize seam bulkiness as shown in Figure A.

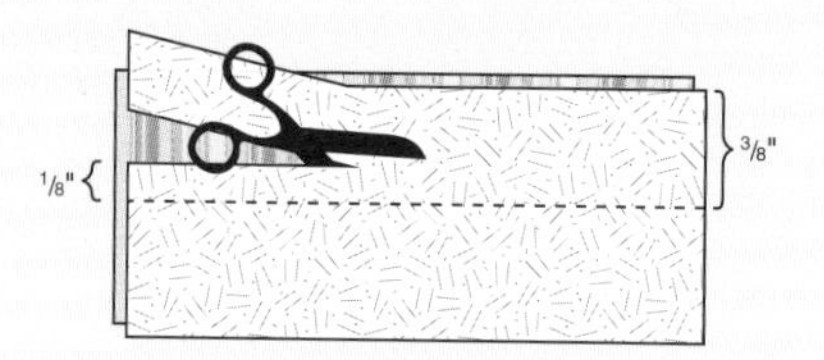

Figure A

Completing the Quilt

1. Layer one B border strip for backing, right side up; add the quilt center, appliquéd side up and matching top 19" edge to strip; second B border strip for quilt front, wrong side up, and batting B referring to Figure 4.

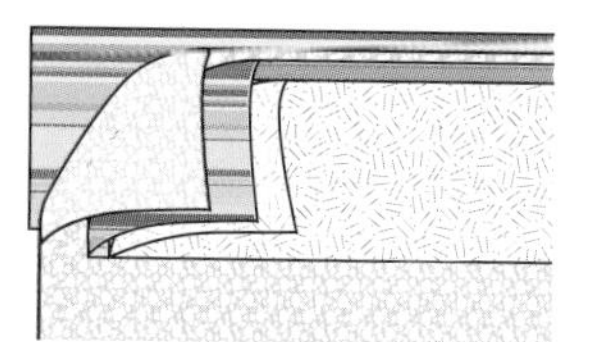

Figure 4

2. Stitch a ½" seam allowance through all layers along 19" edges. Trim batting from seam if necessary.

3. Press border strips and batting away from quilt center matching ends and long edges; pin edges to secure. Carefully trim any excess batting even with border strips.

4. Quilt as desired.

5. Repeat steps 1–4 to attach a B border to the bottom of quilt center.

6. Stitch D squares to short ends of two C border strips using a ½" seam allowance making side borders (Figure 5); press seams toward C. Repeat with remaining C borders and D squares to make backing borders.

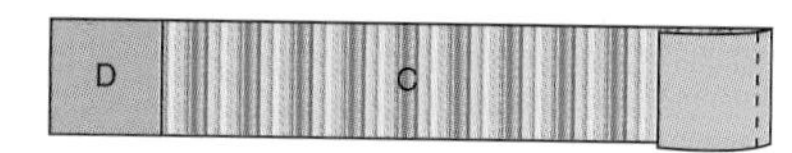

Figure 5

7. Layer, attach and quilt side borders repeating steps 1–4.

8. Stitch H borders together on short ends; press seams to one side. Cut four 5" x 35" H border strips. Stitch I/J borders together on short ends; press seams to one side. Cut four each 5" x 43" I and 5" x 35" J border strips.

9. Continue to add borders to the quilt. Add top and bottom borders first, then side borders repeating steps 1–4 referring to the Placement Diagram for order.

10. Bind quilt using 2¾"-wide binding strips. ■

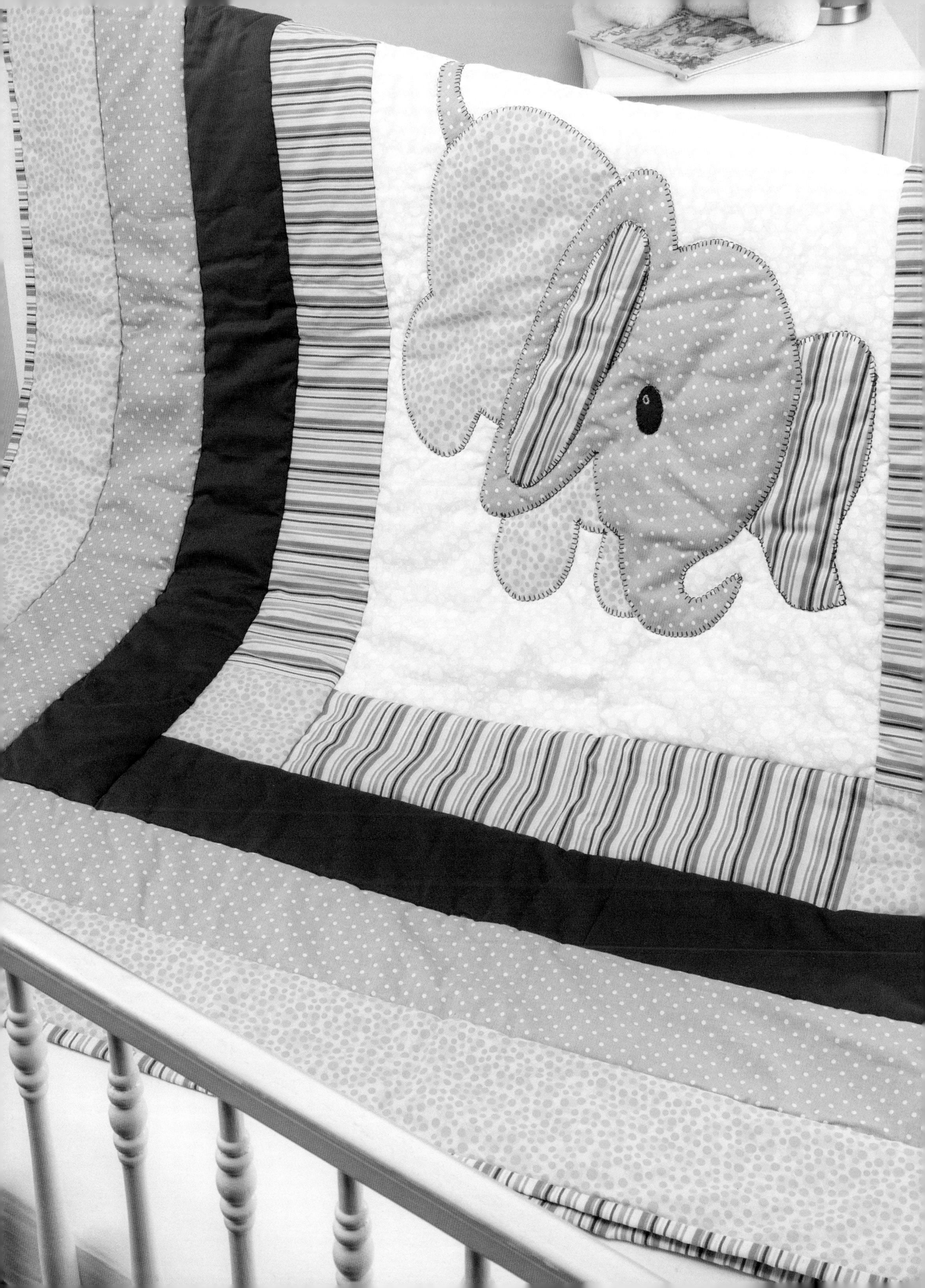

"I have taught this technique for many years, but my concentration toward baby quilts has sky-rocketed since joining the grandma club. I love elephants, they symbolize good luck and I can't think of anything more fitting for a new baby than a beautifully hand-crafted quilt bringing well wishes and love."
—CJ Behling aka CJama

Baby A-Go-Go
Placement Diagram 50" x 56"

Catherine Suggests

This quilt is made with a stitch-and-flip quilt-as-you-go technique. All quilting is done in each border before the next border is added, making the quilt easier to handle during quilting.

If using a low-loft polyester batting, no additional quilting is necessary to secure the batting. So for a quick project, use this type of batting without adding extra quilting. Quilt around the appliqué pieces but do not add extra quilting to the appliquéd center.

If using a cotton or cotton-blend low-loft batting, additional quilting is necessary to stabilize the batting in the quilt. Press the strips away from the quilt and pin as instructed. Stitch 3/8" away from the seam to stabilize the batting (Figure B1). Additional grid or channel quilting can be added as shown in Figure B2 or other quilting patterns as desired.

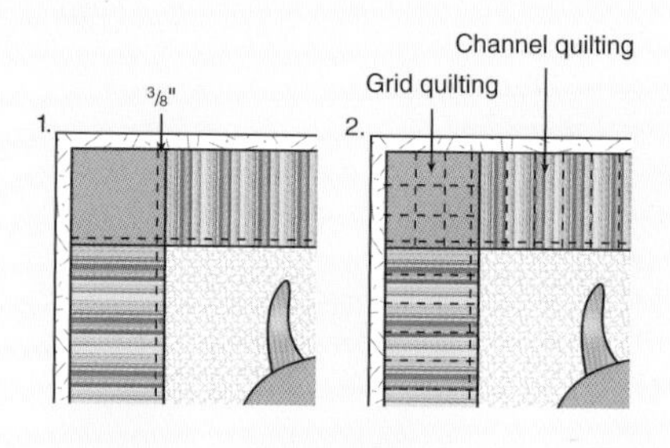

Figure B

Raw-Edge Fusible Appliqué

One of the easiest ways to appliqué is the fusible-web method. Paper-backed fusible web motifs are fused to the wrong side of fabric, cut out and then fused to a foundation fabric and stitched in place by hand or machine. You can use this method for raw- or turned-edge appliqué.

1. If the appliqué motif is directional, it should be reversed for raw-edge fusible appliqué. If doing several identical appliqué motifs, trace reversed motif shapes onto template material to make reusable templates.

2. Use templates or trace the appliqué motif shapes onto paper side of paper-backed fusible web. Leave at least ½" between shapes. Cut out shapes, leaving a margin around traced lines.

3. Follow manufacturer's instructions and fuse shapes to wrong side of fabric as indicated on pattern for color and number to cut.

4. Cut out appliqué shapes on traced lines and remove paper backing from fusible web.

5. Again following manufacturer's instructions, arrange and fuse pieces on the foundation fabric referring to appliqué motif included in pattern.

6. Hand- or machine-stitch around edges. Some stitch possibilities are satin or zigzag, buttonhole, blanket or running stitch. ***Note:*** *Position a light- to medium-weight stabilizer behind the appliqué motif to keep the fabric from puckering during machine stitching.*

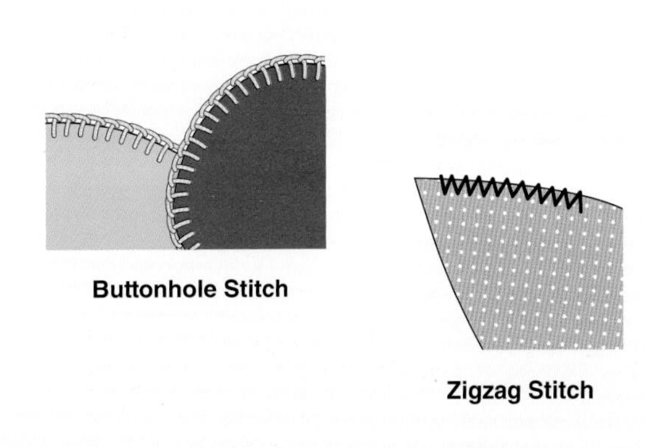

Buttonhole Stitch

Zigzag Stitch

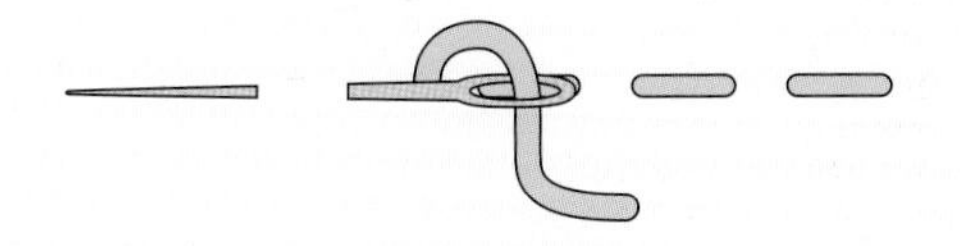

Running Stitch

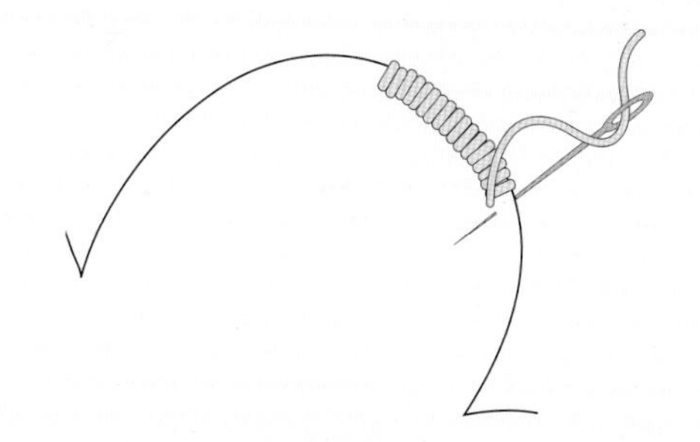

Satin Stitch

Charming Puffy Crib Quilt

Designed & Quilted by Nancy Vasilchik

Make this fun and easy crib quilt for the next baby shower. One side has puffy biscuit blocks, and the other is a rag quilt.

Specifications

Skill Level: Intermediate
Crib Quilt Size: 46" x 50"
Block Size: 4" x 4" Finished
Number of Blocks: 90

Materials

- ½ yard white solid
- ½ yard white flannel
- ⅔ yard pink flannel
- ⅔ yard yellow flannel
- 1 yard yellow print
- 1½ yards blue print
- 1⅝ yards blue flannel
- 1⅔ yards pink print
- 1⅝ yards 45"-wide batting
- Thread
- Polyester fiberfill
- Basic sewing tools and supplies

Cutting

From white solid:

- Cut 4 (2½" by fabric width) C/D border strips.
  Subcut 2 strips into 2 (2½" x 36½") C borders.
  Set aside remaining strips for D borders.

From white flannel:

- Cut 4 (2½" by fabric width) C/D border strips.
  Subcut 2 strips into 2 (2½" x 36½") C borders.
  Set aside remaining strips for D borders.

From pink flannel:

- Cut 4 (5" by fabric width) strips.
  Subcut 30 (5") B squares.

From yellow flannel:

- Cut 4 (5" by fabric width) strips.
  Subcut 30 (5") B squares.

From yellow print:

- Cut 5 (6" by fabric width) strips.
  Subcut 30 (6") A squares.

From blue print:

- Cut 5 (6" by fabric width) strips.
  Subcut 30 (6") A squares.
- Cut 5 (2½" by fabric width) binding strips.

From blue flannel:

- Cut 4 (4½" by fabric length) E/F border strips.
  Subcut 2 strips into 2 (4½" x 39") E borders.
  Set aside remaining strips for F borders.
- Cut 5 (5" by remaining fabric width) strips.
  Subcut 30 (5") B squares.

From pink print:

- Cut 4 (4½" by fabric length) E/F border strips.
  Subcut 2 strips into 2 (4½" x 39") E borders.
  Set aside remaining strips for F borders.
- Cut 6 (6" by remaining fabric width) strips.
  Subcut 30 (6") A squares.

From batting:

- Cut 4 (2½" by fabric width) strips.
  Subcut 2 (2½" x 36") C borders and 2 (2½" x 43") D borders.
- Cut 4 (4½" by fabric length) strips.
  Subcut 2 each 4½" x 50" F borders and 4½" x 39" E borders.

Assembly

1. Pin the corners of an A square to the corners of a same color flannel B square, wrong sides together and referring to Figure 1.

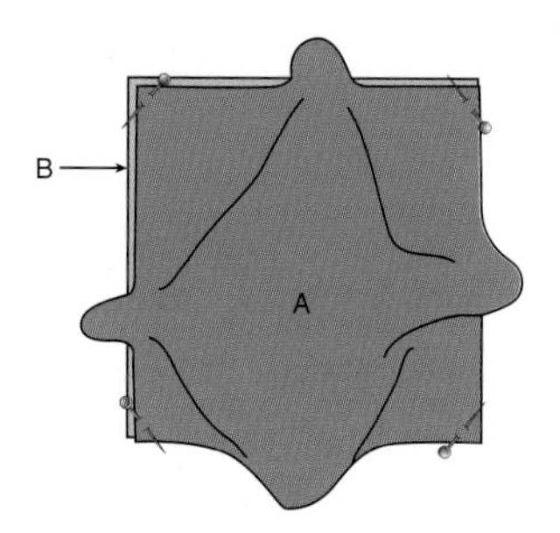

Figure 1

Ugly Duckling

2. Fold and pin a ½" pleat into three sides of A, taking up the extra fabric to match the B side length referring to Figure 2. Fold pleats in same direction. Hand- or machine-baste ⅜" from pleated sides to secure.

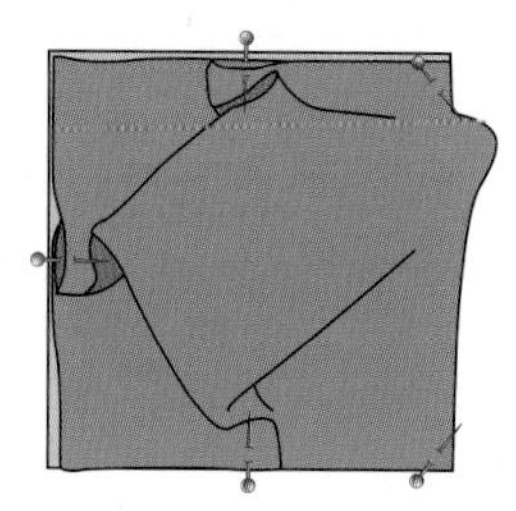

Figure 2

3. Insert polyester fiberfill into the open side to softly fill the pouch.

Nancy Suggests

Overfilling the pouch will make it more difficult to stitch the blocks together. Softly stuff the pouch beginning with a small handful of fiberfill and adding small amounts to the desired fullness.

4. Fold and stitch a ½" pleat into the fourth side of the block and baste to complete one Biscuit and Rag block (Figure 3).

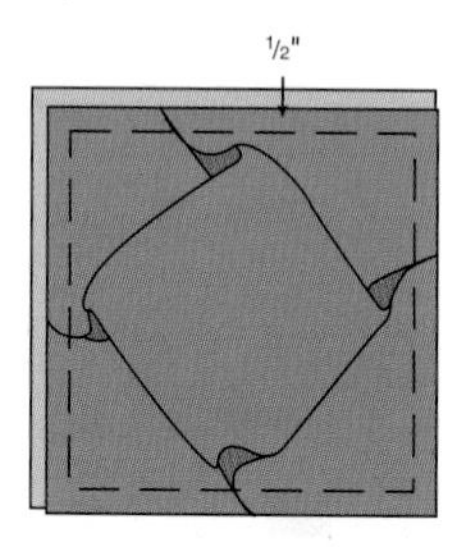

Figure 3

5. Repeat steps 1–4 to make 30 each pink, blue and yellow blocks.

6. Arrange blocks in 10 rows of nine blocks each referring to the Front Placement Diagram or as desired.

7. Pin two adjacent blocks, puffy right sides together. Using a ½" seam allowance, stitch blocks together (Figure 4).

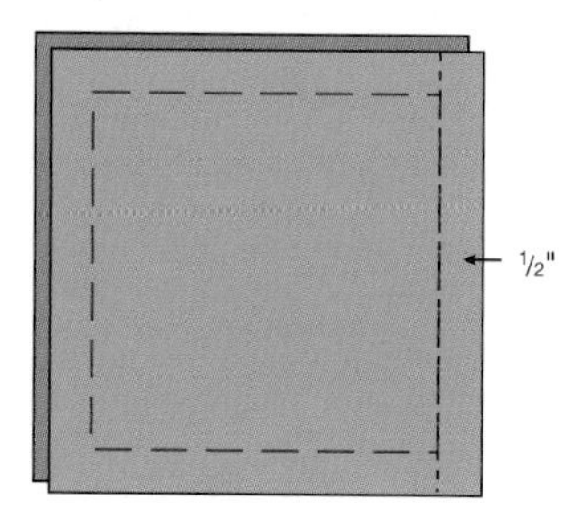

Figure 4

Nancy Suggests

Since blocks are puffy, more guiding and compressing is required than when sewing flat fabric.

Use a zipper foot to stitch the blocks together. It will make stitching close to the puffy pouch easier.

Use a short stitch length to keep the fiberfill from creeping out of the stitches.

8. Stitch remaining blocks together in rows as arranged.

9. Pin and stitch rows together as arranged, pinning seam allowances in opposite directions and nesting seams to complete quilt center (Figure 5).

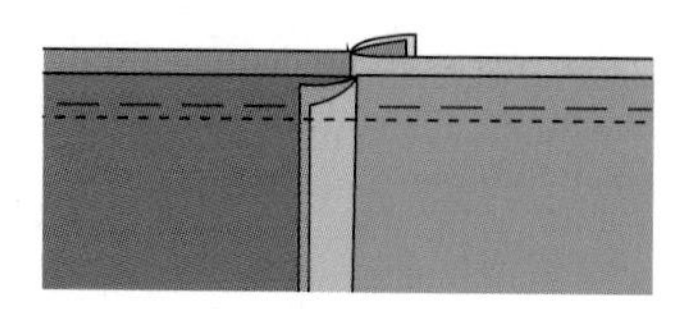

Figure 5

10. Remove basting stitches around blocks when rows are joined.

11. Baste ⅜" from quilt center outer edges, stitching row and block seams open.

12. Stitch white solid D strips together on short ends; press seams open. Subcut two 2½" x 44½" D borders. Repeat with white flannel D strips.

13. Position white flannel C along top edge of flannel/rag wrong side of quilt center and white solid C, right side down on puffy right side of quilt center, with batting C on top; pin together (Figure 6).

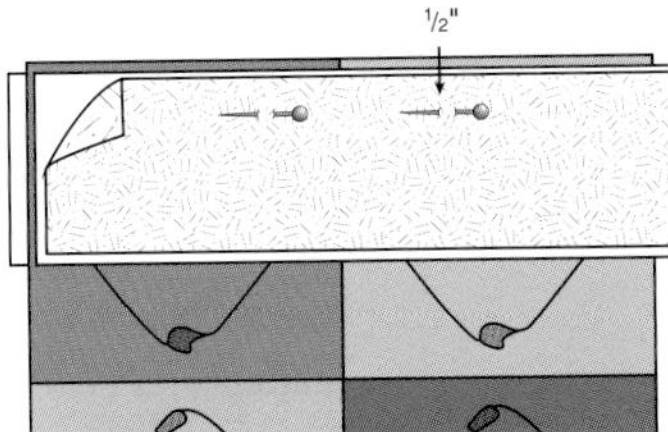

Figure 6

14. Stitch through all layers using a ½" seam allowance. Press C layers away from quilt center and baste together ⅜" from opposite edge.

15. Attach a C border to bottom of quilt center and D borders to opposite sides, repeating steps 12 and 13.

16. Attach an E border to top and bottom of quilt and F borders to opposite sides in the same manner.

17. Prepare binding and bind quilt, mitering corners.

18. To complete flannel/rag side of quilt, clip seam allowances approximately every ¼–⅜" being careful not to clip through seams. Wash the quilt to make seam allowances curl. ■

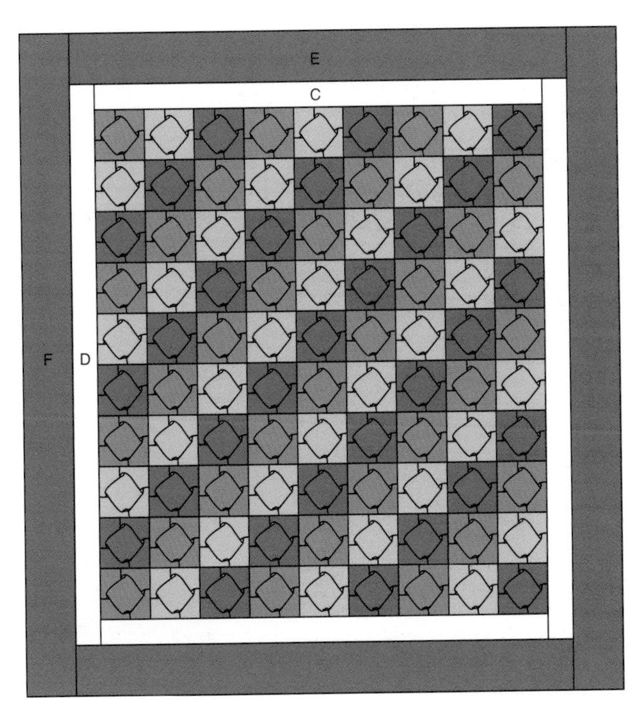

Charming Puffy Crib Quilt (Front)
Placement Diagram 46" x 50"

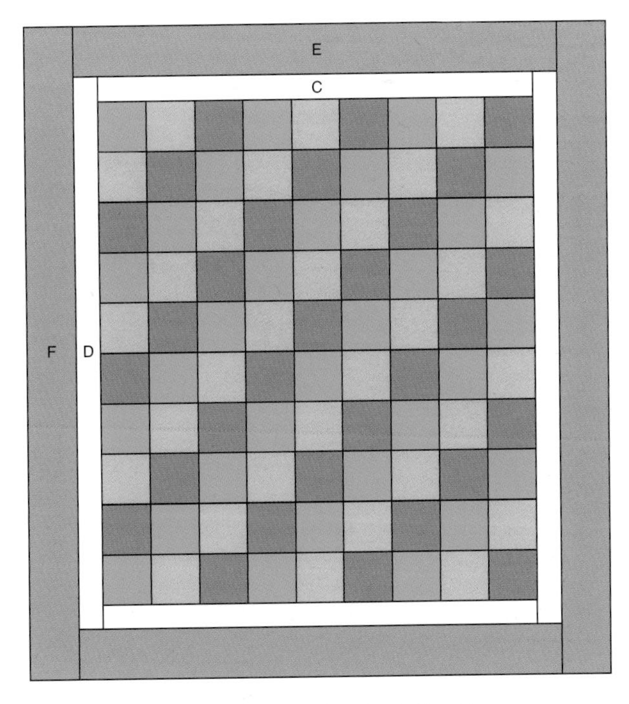

Charming Puffy Crib Quilt (Back)
Placement Diagram 46" x 50"

KATHY CANO
MURILLO

Ready, Set, Go Bag

Designed & Quilted by Jenny Rekeweg

Keep your scraps handy and work on these adorable bags when you have a few extra minutes. Use as personalized gift bags or for sorting. One will never be enough.

Specifications

Skill Level: Confident Beginner
Bag Size: 9" x 12" x 4"

Materials

- Fat quarters or large scraps 3–5 different black-with-white prints
- ¼ yard red print
- ½ yard lining
- ½ yard batting
- Thread
- Even-feed or walking presser foot
- Basic sewing tools and supplies

Jenny Suggests

This project is very scrap friendly. Cut bag strips from larger scraps or piece scraps together and then cut. Use a favorite or themed print for the bag top band.

Don't stress over the width of the strips. Cut whatever appeals to you and keep adding strips to the base until it is covered. Rulers only provide straight edges to roll your rotary cutter along!

Even the batting base can be made from scraps. Piece batting scraps together with a wide zigzag stitch. Be sure the batting scraps are a similar fabric content.

Cutting

From black-with-white prints:

- Cut a total of 10–14 strips 2½"–3½" wide by 12" long.
- Cut 2 (6" x 18") rectangles for bag top band from same print.

From red print:

- Cut 2 (2" by fabric width) strips.
  Subcut 4 (2" x 12") strips for quilting.
  Set aside remainder of second strip for drawstring.

From lining:

- Cut 1 (15" by fabric width) strip.
  Subcut 2 (13" x 15") rectangles.

From batting:

- Cut 1 (16" by fabric width) strip.
  Subcut 2 (16" x 18") rectangles.

Assembly

1. Mark a vertical centerline and a horizontal line across a batting rectangle 6" down from the 16" edge referring to Figure 1.

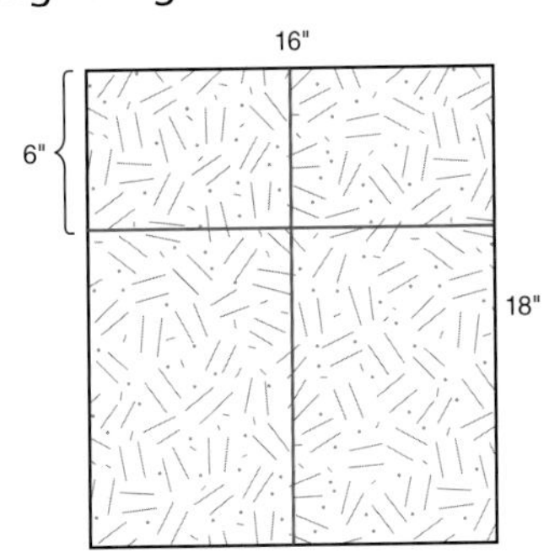

Figure 1

2. Position a black-with-white print strip right side up at the middle of the batting rectangle along the vertical center line between the marked horizontal line and the bottom of the batting rectangle.

3. Position and pin a second black-with-white print strip right sides together on the first strip. Stitch ¼"–⅜" away from vertical center edges (Figure 2). Press second strip away from first.

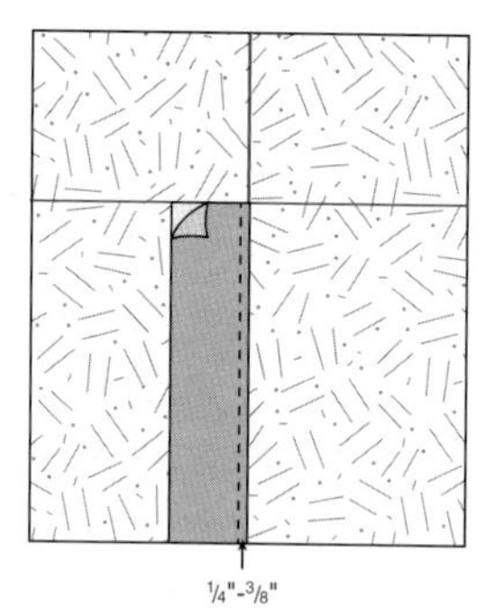

Figure 2

4. Quilt each strip separately as desired (Figure 3).

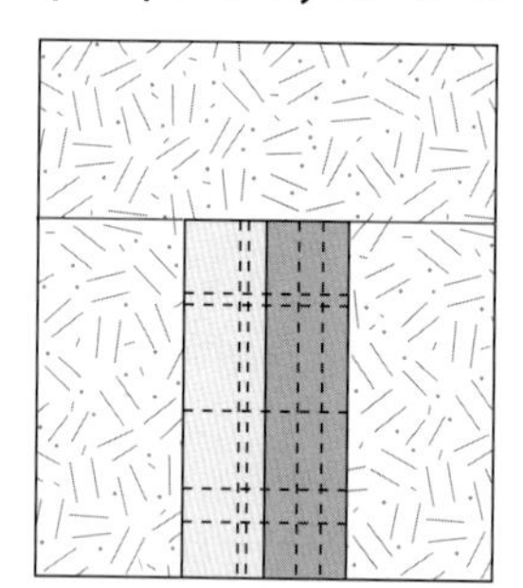

Figure 3

Jenny Suggests

Like all small projects, this one gives you the chance to experiment with and practice quilting patterns. Quilt each strip differently before adding another strip. Your bag will be a palette of quilting choices and how they work with each other.

5. Add strips to either side of the first strips, repeating steps 3 and 4. Add 2" x 12" red strips last to either side or as desired.

6. Stitch the bag top band right side down across the strips matching one long edge along the marked horizontal line. Press away from strips and quilt as desired to complete bag front.

7. Trim completed bag front to 13" x 15" making sure the horizontal seam is 4½" from the top edge as shown in Figure 4.

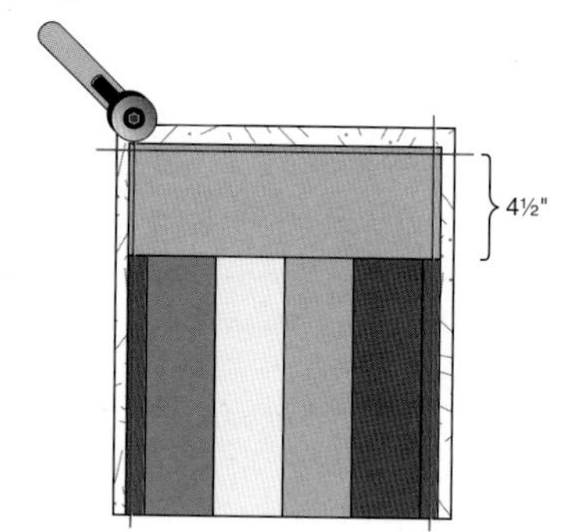

Figure 4

8. Repeat steps 1–7 to complete the quilted bag back.

9. Stitch a lining rectangle and quilted bag front right sides together along the 13" top edges (Figure 5). Press seam toward lining.

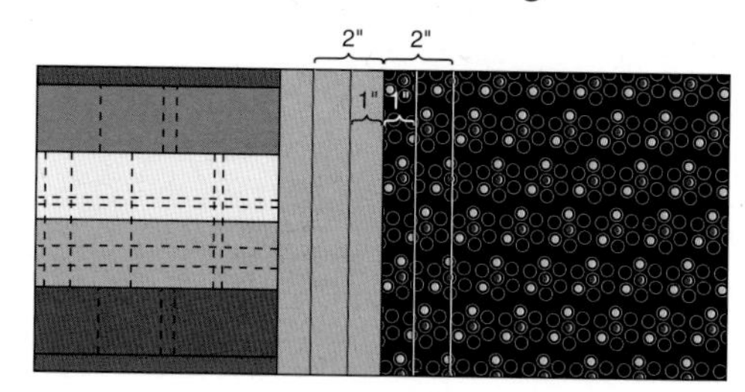

Figure 5

10. Mark two stitching placement lines 1" and 2" from seam on the lining and bag front referring to red lines on Figure 5 for drawstring casing.

11. Repeat steps 9 and 10 with second lining and bag back.

12. Pin bag/lining front to bag/lining back right sides together matching seams and bag and lining fronts to backs.

13. Stitch together around perimeter. Leave the seam open between the stitching placement lines on one side of the bag top, backstitching at the

1" and 2" lines as shown in Figure 6, and leave a 3" opening in the bottom lining seam for turning.

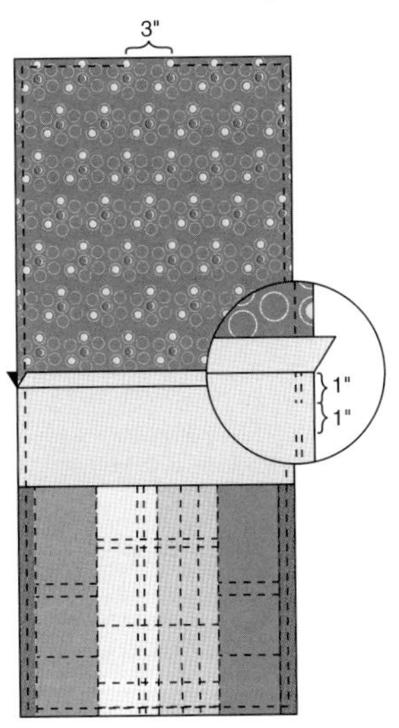

Figure 6

14. Press side seams open.

15. To box bottom corners for a flat bottom, fold a side seam to form a point. Mark a stitching line 2" from the point and stitch (Figure 7). Trim seam allowance to ¼". Repeat on all lining and bag corners.

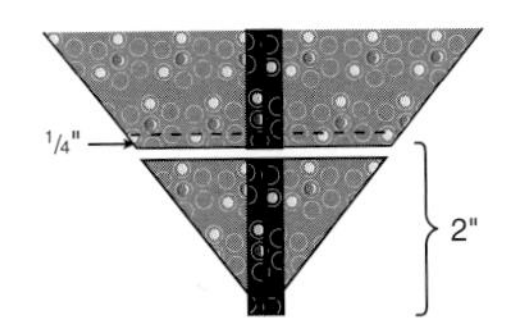

Figure 7

16. Turn right side out through lining opening. Stitch lining opening closed. Push lining into bag and press top edge flat.

17. Pin and stitch through all layers along marked stitching lines at top of bag to create drawstring casing. **Note:** *Opening left in bag side seam should be between the stitching lines.*

18. Referring to Figure 8, fold and press both short ends of remaining 2"-wide red strip ¼" to wrong side. Fold and press strip in half wrong sides together. Unfold and press long sides to center; re-press in half. Edgestitch both long edges and across both ends to make drawstring.

19. Thread drawstring into casing through side seam opening. Tie knots in drawstring ends. ■

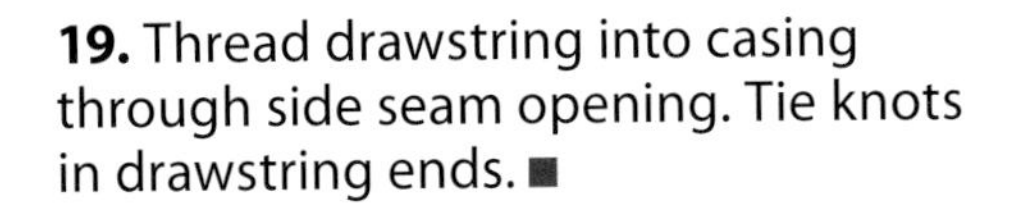

Figure 8

"I was inspired by the black and white because of our soccer practices. My son loves the skull and cross bones print! I already plan to make another bag for my daughter to keep her ballet stuff ready and all together." —Jenny Rekeweg

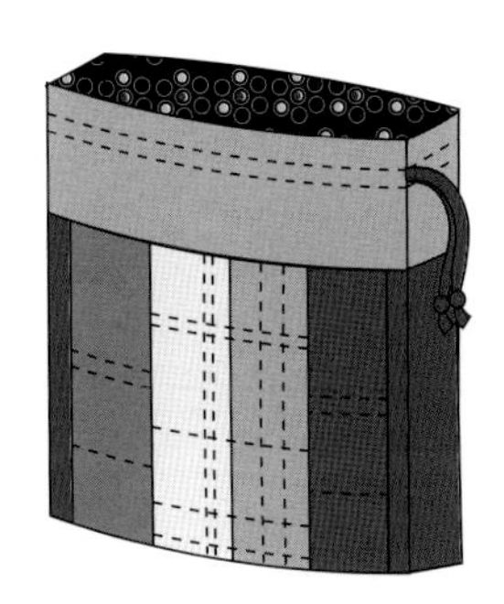

Ready, Set, Go Bag
Placement Diagram 9" x 12" x 4"

Dine O Mite

Designed & Quilted by Ann Lauer

Bargello quilts look intricate but are actually easy to make. This mirror-image bargello design creates negative space for appliqué. Using strip piecing, stitch-and-flip quilting, some simple appliqué and a bit of embellishment, you can create your own table runner.

Specifications

Skill Level: Intermediate
Table Runner Size: 48" x 24"

Materials

- ⅝ yard medium red tonal
- ⅓ yard dark red tonal
- ⅓ yard white solid
- ⅞ yard black solid
- 1¾ yards backing
- 1¾ yards 45"-wide batting
- Thread
- Fusible preprinted quilting grid, 54" x 28" (optional)
- ½ yard paper-backed fusible web
- Fabric basting spray (optional)
- Package 3mm hot fix crystals and applicator (optional)
- Nonstick appliqué pressing sheet
- Even-feed or walking presser foot
- Basic sewing tools and supplies

Cutting

From medium red tonal:
- Cut 7 (2½" by fabric width) strips. Set aside 4 strips for binding.
- Cut appliqué pieces as per patterns and instructions.

From dark red tonal:
- Cut 3 (2½" by fabric width) strips.

From white solid:
- Cut 3 (2½" by fabric width) strips.
- Cut appliqué pieces as per patterns and instructions.

From black solid:
- Cut 9 (2½" by fabric width) strips.

From backing:
- Cut 1 (28" by fabric length) strip. Subcut 1 (54" x 28") rectangle.

From batting:
- Cut 1 (28" by fabric length) strip. Subcut 1 (54" x 28") rectangle.

Preparing Quilt Base

1. Layer batting rectangle on top of backing rectangle for quilt base. Pin-, thread- or spray-baste layers together.

2. Mark a vertical line 2" from left edge of quilt base (Figure 1). Continue marking vertical lines 4" apart across width.

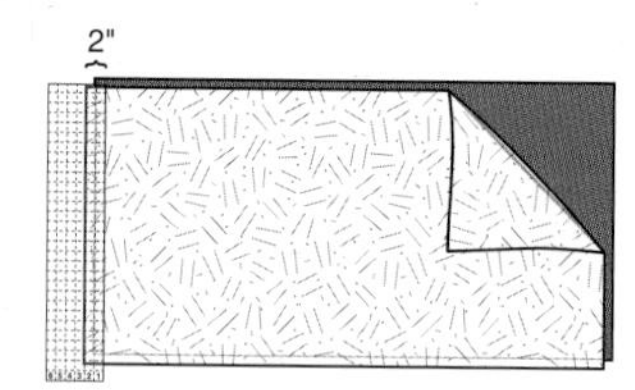

Figure 1

Ann Suggests

You can use a preprinted fusible grid. Position it so that a horizontal line is even with the top of the fabric and a vertical line is even with the left edge.

The grid lines should not show through the fabric. If using light-color fabrics, apply the grid to the backing fabric and lay the batting on top of the grid. You should be able to see the grid lines through the batting but not through lighter-color fabrics.

3. Mark a horizontal line 2" from quilt base top. Continue marking horizontal lines 4" apart across length creating a grid as shown in Figure 2.

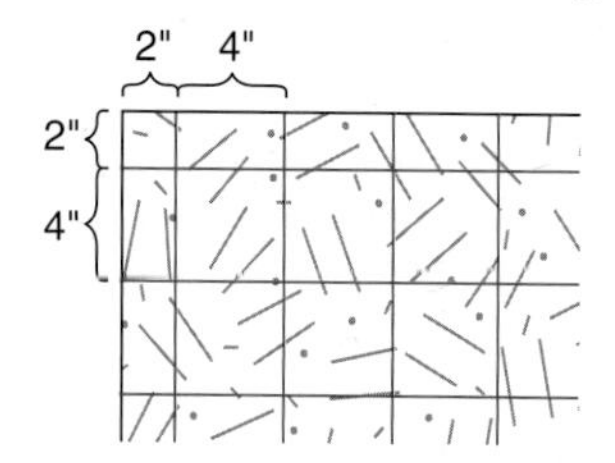

Figure 2

Ann Suggests

Use a water-soluble fabric marking pen or one that disappears when heat is applied for marking grid lines. You don't want them to show through light-color fabrics when the table runner is completed.

Preparing Strip Sets

1. Select one each white, dark red and medium red strips, and three black strips. Arrange strips in order shown in Figure 3.

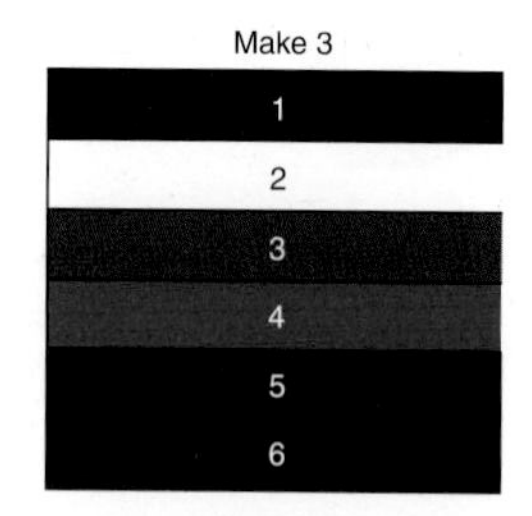

Figure 3

Ann Suggests

Stitch with even-numbered strips on top and odd-numbered strips on bottom. This means that when stitching pairs together, you will flip them over and stitch from the opposite end. This helps keep the strip sets straight. As you stitch strip pairs together, keep them even on one end.

Don't pull the strips as you stitch. Pulling the strips through the machine stretches them.

2. Stitch strips together in pairs along length; then stitch pairs together, keeping ends even at one end of the strip set. Repeat to make three strip sets.

3. Press seams in one strip set toward strip 1 and label as set A. Press seams in second strip set toward strip 2 and label as set B. Label the third strip set as set C; do not press C seams at this time.

4. Stitch set A strip 6 to strip 1 creating a tube (Figure 4). Press seam in same direction as other seams. Repeat for sets B and C.

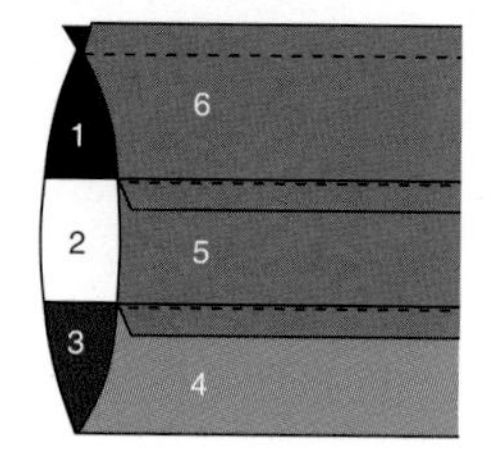

Figure 4

Completing Bargello Quilt Center

1. Lay A and B tubes on cutting mat, carefully folding flat on seam lines.

2. Cut a 3½"-wide section from each A and B tube (Figure 5).

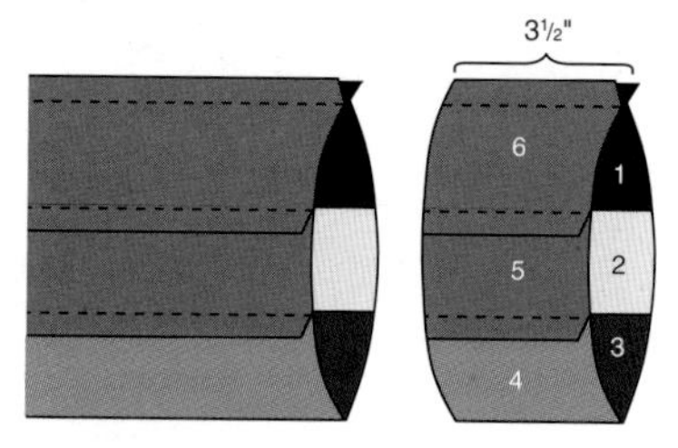

Figure 5

3. Remove the stitching between strips 1 and 6 from each cut section (Figure 6).

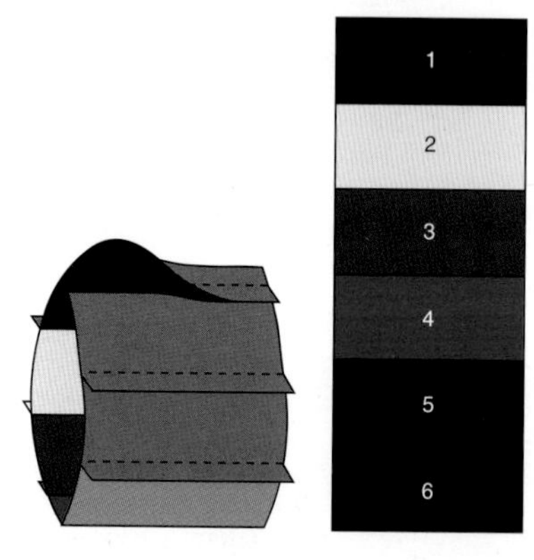

Figure 6

4. Turn B section upside down and stitch A and B sections together along the strip 6 edges referring to Figure 7 to complete segment 1. Seams should all be pressed toward strip 1. ***Note:*** *Same-color strips will be stitched together each time the A and B sections are joined.*

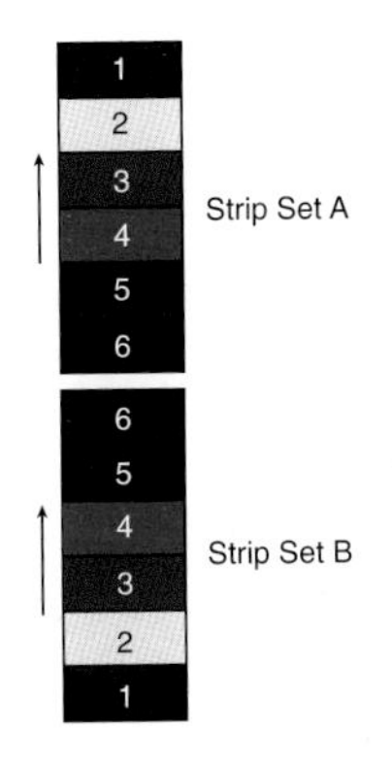

Figure 7

5. Position segment 1 wrong side down on quilt base matching edges to left and top edges of grid (Figure 8). Baste in place ⅛" from left edge referring again to Figure 8.

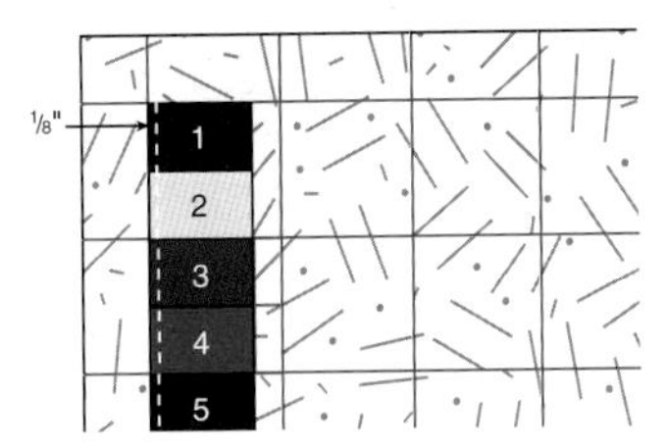

Figure 8

6. Cut a 2½" section from each A and B tube. Remove the stitching between strips 5 and 6. Turn B section upside down and stitch A and B sections together along the strip 5 edges to complete segment 2. Seams should all be pressed toward strip 2.

7. Flip segment 2 end for end. Position and pin right sides together on segment 1, nesting seams and matching edges on unstitched side (Figure 9a). Stitch long edge and press segment 2 away from segment 1; pin unsewn edge in place (Figure 9b).

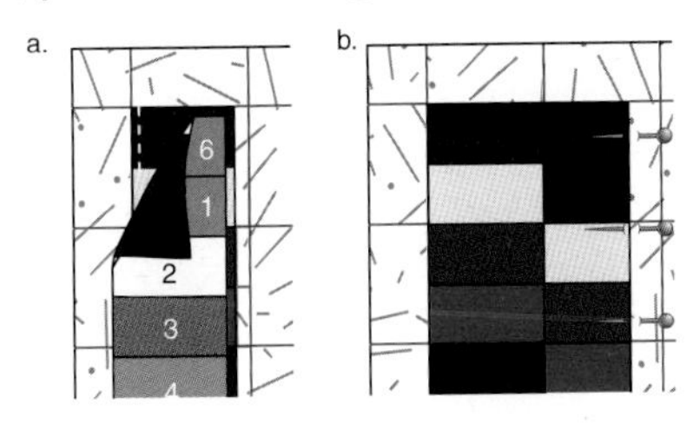

Figure 9

Ann Suggests

As you attach each new segment, pin carefully and check with the grid lines to be certain the seam lines are horizontal. If the segments are beginning to slant or bow, make slight adjustments as soon as possible.

8. Repeat steps 2–7, with sections 3–13 from A and B tubes to make segments. Add segments across the quilt base. Refer to Figure 10 for section widths to cut and where to open the tubes.

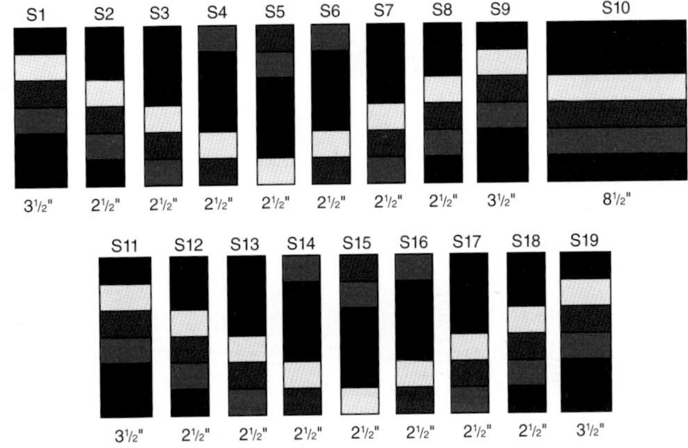

Figure 10

9. Cut two of each section from C tube to prepare and add segments 14–19, referring to steps 2–7 and Figure 10. Press segment seams in opposite directions segment to segment to nest seams when adding a segment.

10. Stitch ⅛" from right edge of segment 19 to secure.

Completing the Table Runner

1. Square and straighten the completed table runner as needed.

2. Bind the table runner with 2½"-wide strips referring to Mitered Corner Binding on page 30 using a ⅜" seam allowance.

3. Prepare large and small half-heart appliqué pieces using patterns given on the pattern insert and referring to Raw-Edge Fusible Appliqué on page 17.

4. Remove paper backing and overlap red half-heart edges over white half-heart edges on nonstick appliqué pressing sheet (Figure 11); press. Make four large hearts and six small hearts.

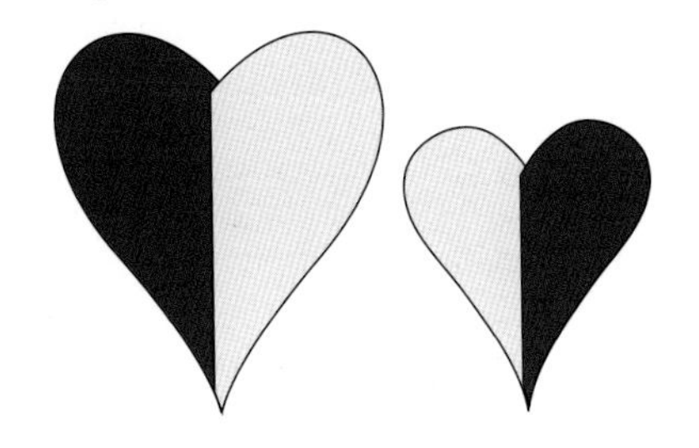
Figure 11

5. Layer a small heart centered on a large heart on the nonstick appliqué pressing sheet (Figure 12); press. Make four layered hearts.

Figure 12

6. Referring to Placement Diagram and photo, position and fuse layered hearts in table runner center and small hearts on ends. Stitch around heart edges as desired.

7. If desired, apply hot-fix crystals to table runner referring to manufacturer's instructions. ■

"I'm always looking for a new twist for bargello projects. This mirror image technique provides a perfect backdrop to showcase the appliqué motifs." —Ann Lauer

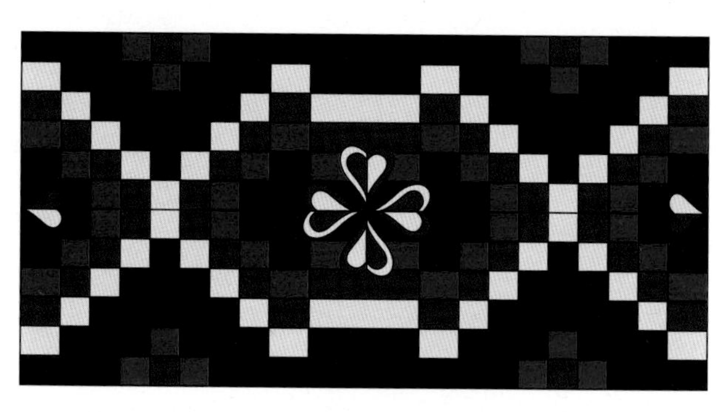

Dine O Mite
Placement Diagram 48" x 24"

Mitered Corner Binding

Binding your quilt completes the quilting process. As with all quilting techniques, there are many choices of ways to bind your quilt. The following are instructions for a continuous, double-fold binding with mitered corners and overlapped ends. Check in a complete quilting guide for other techniques.

1. Join binding strips on short ends with diagonal seams to make one long strip; trim seams to ¼" and press seams open (Figure A).

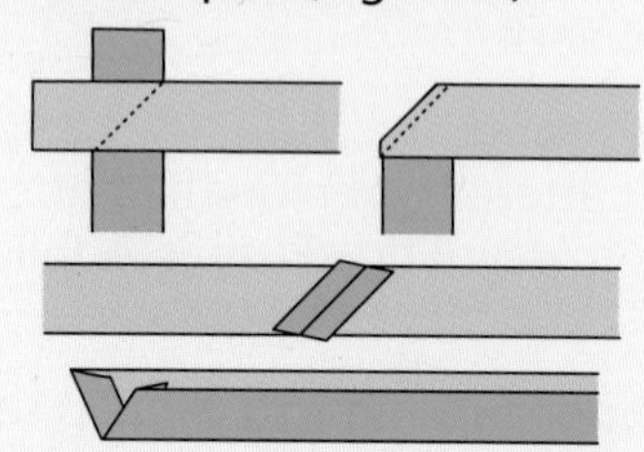

Figure A

2. Fold 1" of one short end to wrong side and press. Fold the binding strip in half with wrong sides together along length, again referring to Figure A; press.

3. Starting 3" from the folded short end, sew binding to quilt top edges, matching raw edges and using a ¼" seam. Stop stitching ¼" from corner and backstitch (Figure B).

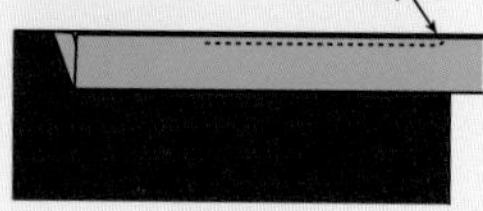

Figure B

4. Fold binding up at a 45-degree angle to seam and then down even with quilt edges, forming a pleat at corner, referring to Figure C.

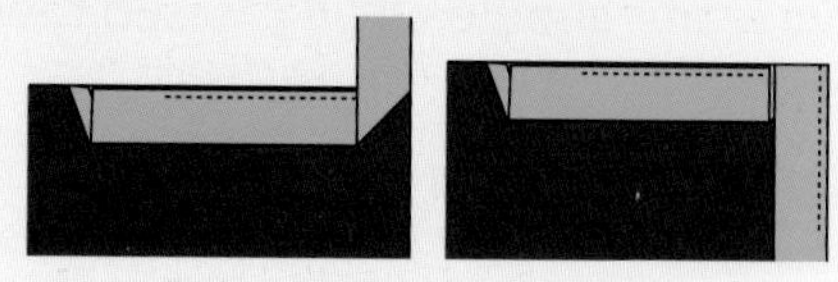

Figure C

5. Resume stitching from corner edge as shown in Figure 6, down quilt side, backstitching ¼" from next corner. Repeat, mitering all corners, stitching to within 3" of starting point.

6. Trim binding end long enough to tuck inside starting end and complete stitching (Figure D).

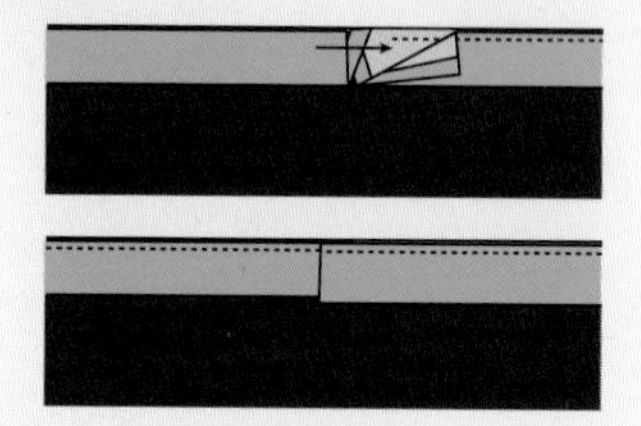

Figure D

7. Fold binding to quilt back and stitch in place by hand or machine to complete your quilt.

Bargello Notes

Bargello is a quilting style that copies the European bargello needlepoint embroidery style from the Middle Ages used on pillows, upholstery and carpets. The design is geometric and created by using many hues of color producing intricate shaded waves or flames across the pieces.

In quilting, the pattern of waves or flames in bargello is created when horizontal strip sets are made, cut again into vertical strips, and then offset.

- Strip sets are made from same-width strips cut the width of the fabric (Figure A).

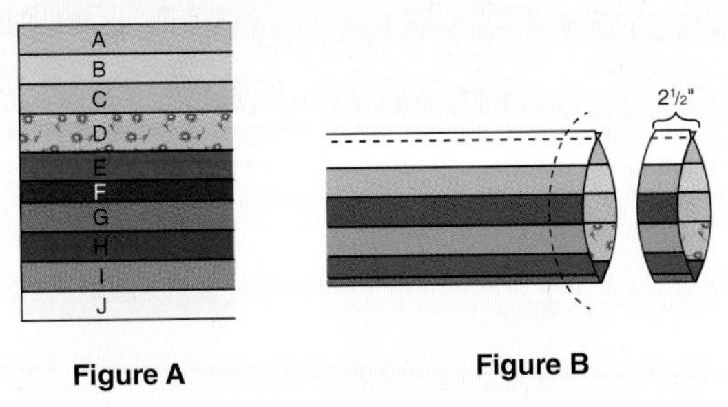

Figure A **Figure B**

The sets are stitched into tubes and the tubes are cut into different-size sections (Figure B).

The tubes are then opened at different seams to create vertical strips. The vertical strips are arranged so that the colors in adjacent strips appear to step up or down by the width of one color segment, creating a wave of the same color across the piece (Figure C).

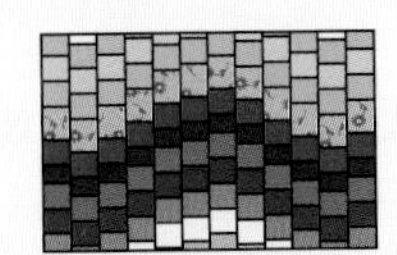

Figure C

Strip sets can also be made from strips of different widths cut the width of the fabric to create even more variety in the final design.

- Strip sets do not need to be stitched into tubes. Cut vertical strips from the strip sets and arrange several strips on a flat surface, offsetting adjacent strips by no more than one color segment to create the pattern desired (Figure D).

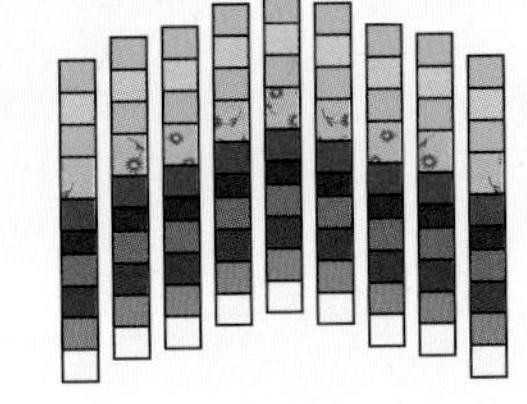

Figure D

Open seams between color segments at the top and bottom of the strips and reattach to even the length of the vertical strips. Then arrange another group of strips to continue the design (Figure E).

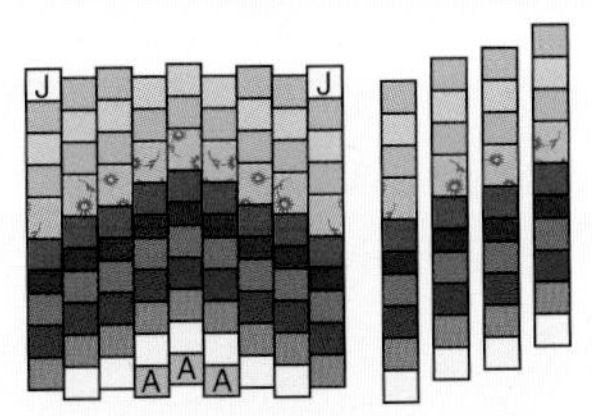

Figure E

The quilt will need to be squared and straightened on top and bottom when using this technique so the strip sets will need to be much longer than the completed size (Figure F).

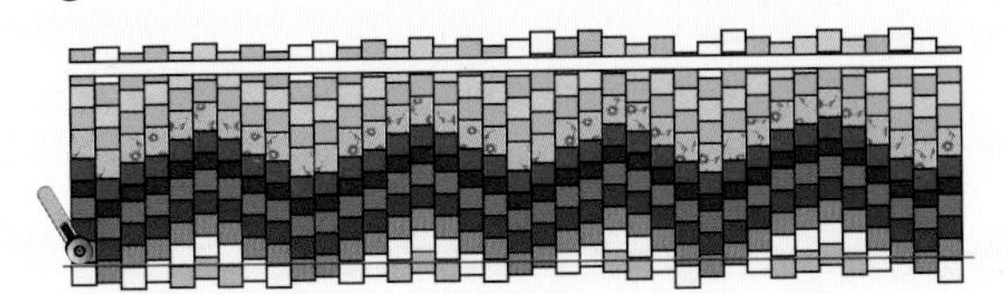

Figure F

Bargello quilts require several levels of planning to achieve even a simple wave pattern. Here are a few helpful hints.

- Charting out the colors and strip widths on grid paper or quilting software makes construction easier.
- Label strip sets and segments when designing.
- Be sure to label strip sets and segments as they are constructed.
- Stitch strips sets together in pairs and then stitch the pairs together in opposite directions to keep sets straight and square.
- Press seams in segments in opposite directions, segment to segment, so that seams can be nested.
- Fabrics should never shift up or down more than one color segment at a time to create the wave movement. Sometimes a shift of less than one color segment, will create an even more pleasing pattern.

Fresh Fruit Table Topper

Designed and Quilted by Tricia Lynn Maloney

If you start now, adding strips to the center square using a stitch-and-flip technique, this cute table topper will be ready for this evening's meal!

Specifications

Skill Level: Confident Beginner
Table Topper Size: 24" x 24"

Materials

- 1 fat eighth red apple print
- 1 fat quarter fruit print
- ⅜ yard green apple print
- ⅝ yard red print
- Batting 28" x 28"
- Backing 28" x 28"
- Thread
- Basic sewing tools and supplies

Cutting

From red apple print:

- Cut 1 (8½") A square.

From fruit print:

- Cut 2 (2½" by fabric width) strips.
  Subcut into 1 (2½" x 12½") F, 2 (2½/" x 14½") G/H and 1 (2½" x 16½") I strips.

From green apple print:

- Cut 4 (2½" by fabric width) strips.
  Subcut 1 each 2½" x20½" N and 2½" x 24½" Q strips.
  Subcut 2 (2½" x 22½") O/P.

From red print:

- Cut 4 (2½" by fabric width) strips.
  Subcut 1 each 2½" x 8½" B, 2½" x 12½" E, 2½" x 16½" J and 2½" x 20½" M strips.
  Subcut 2 each 2½" x 10½" C/D and 2½" x 18½" K/L strips.
- Cut 3 (2¼" by fabric width) strips for binding.

Tricia Suggests

Of course, pick fabrics that you love, but if you are using busy prints together, repeat one semisolid fabric to calm the design down.

Assembly

1. Layer the backing fabric wrong side up with batting centered on top and pin or thread-baste together.

2. Mark lines on both diagonals on the batting.

3. Carefully fold A in half on both diagonals to mark the center. Position A on the batting, matching centers; pin A in place (Figure 1).

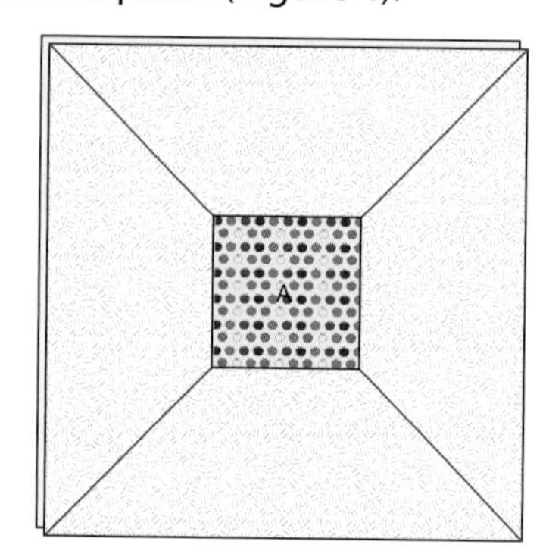

Figure 1

4. Position and pin B on the left-hand side of A, right sides together (Figure 2). Stitch using a ¼" seam allowance, backstitching at beginning and end of seam to secure.

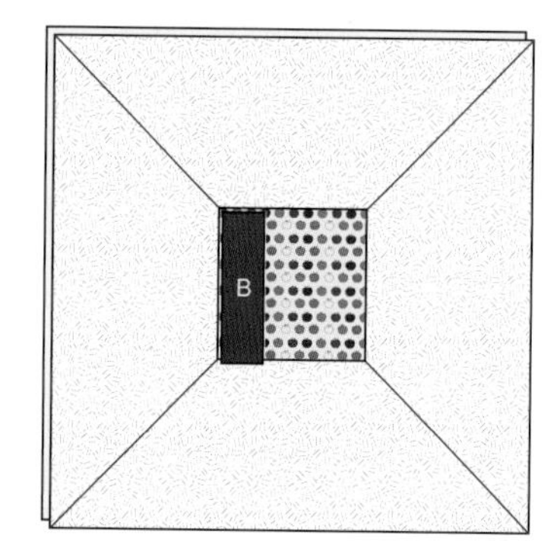

Figure 2

5. Press B away from A.

6. Position C, right sides together, on A-B at top of A (Figure 3). Stitch together, backstitching at beginning and end of seam. Press C away from A-B.

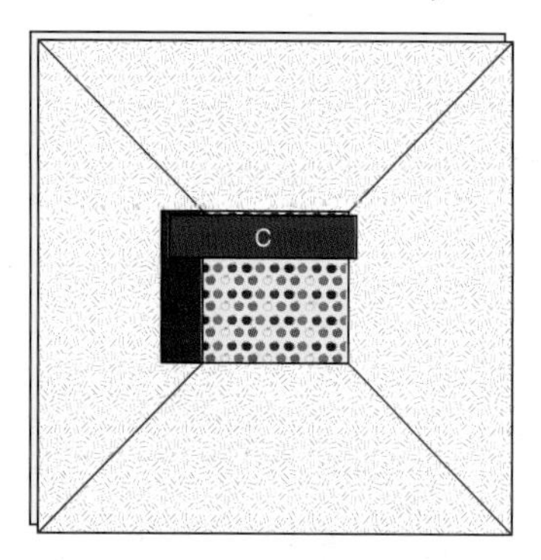

Figure 3

7. Position and stitch D to the right-hand side of A-B-C unit and press away from A (Figure 4).

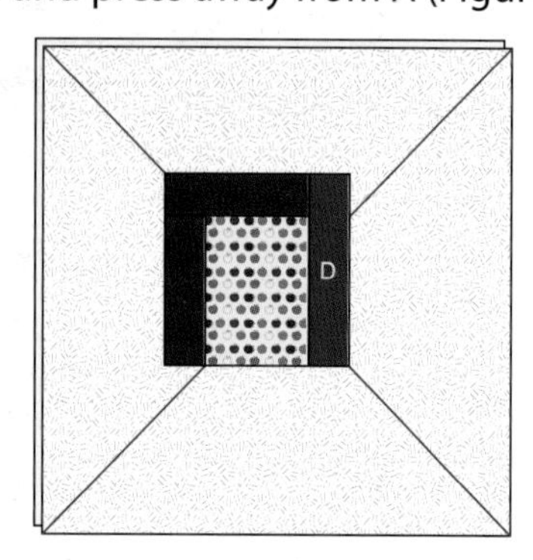

Figure 4

8. Position and stitch E to the bottom of A-B-C-D unit and press away from A (Figure 5).

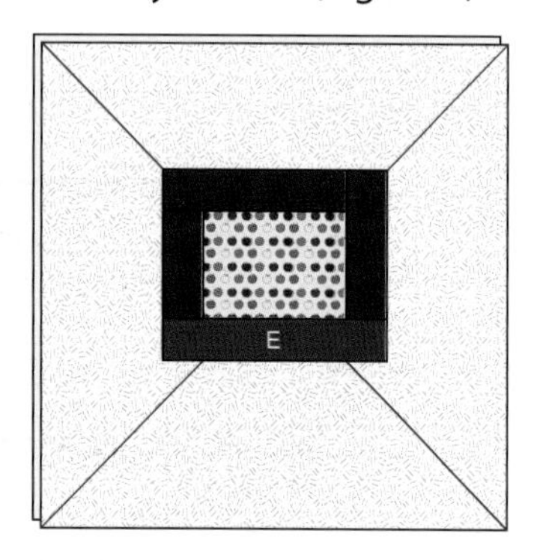

Figure 5

9. Continue to stitch and flip strips in alphabetical order around A referring to Figure 6.

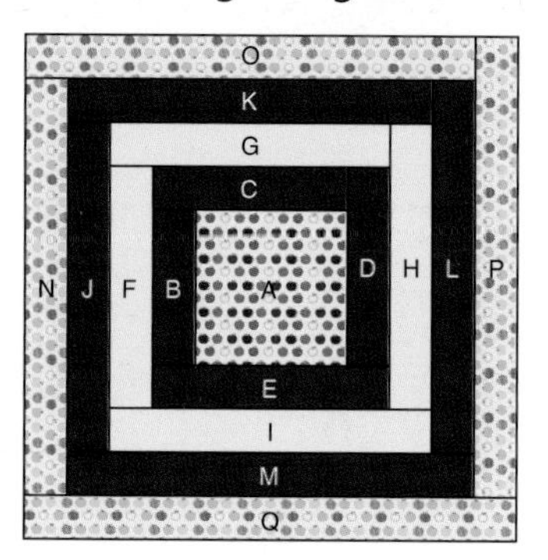

Figure 6

10. Trim excess backing and batting even with stitched unit.

11. Bind with 2¼" binding strips to complete the table topper. ■

"Simple blocks and scrumptious fabrics ...OH MY! This collection of fabrics really inspired me to create a fast, fun table topper that could be completed in a matter of hours!" —Tricia Lynn Maloney

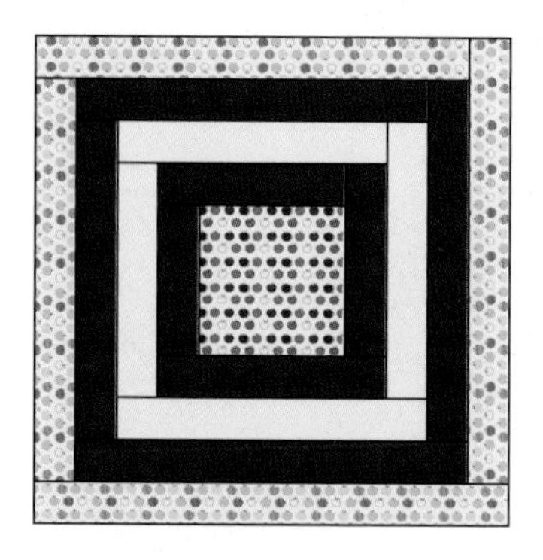

Fresh Fruit Table Topper
Placement Diagram 24" x 24"

Paint Box Squares

Designed & Quilted by Chris Malone

This is a great take-along project once you have assembled the blocks. Stitch connecting strips by machine or hand, and then finish the back sashing when you have time to kill at appointments or in the car.

Specifications

Skill Level: Intermediate
Quilt Size: 57½" x 57½"
Block Size: 9" x 9" finished
Number of Blocks: 36

Materials

- Assorted scraps tonals and single-color prints
- 1⅛ yard white tonal
- 2 yards black with multicolored dots
- 2⅞ yards backing
- 2⅞ yards batting
- Size 12 or 16 pearl cotton to match fabrics
- Thread
- Walking or even-feed presser foot
- Basic sewing tools and supplies

Chris Suggests

This is a great design to use up leftover precuts or scraps, including precut 5" squares for the blocks and precut 10" squares for the backing. Make a completely scrappy back or incorporate a precut 10" square package to make the quilt reversible.

Cutting

From assorted scraps tonals & single-color prints:

- Cut 144 (5") A squares in groups of four in same color family.

From white tonal:

- Cut 10 (2¾" by fabric width) strips.
  Subcut 144 (2¾") B squares.

From black with multicolored dots:

Note: *Cut in order listed.*

- Cut 6 (2¼" by fabric width) strips along crosswise grain for binding.
- Cut 5 (1⅛" x 58") F strips and 5 (1¾" x 58") E strips along fabric length.
- Cut 4 (9½" by remaining fabric width) strips.
  Subcut 30 each 1⅛" x 9½" D and 1¾" x 9½" C strips.

Chris Suggests

Cut E/F binding-and-connecting strips after cutting outer binding strips. The length of these strips may require adjustment after construction and measurement of the rows.

Cut the C and D block binding-and-connecting strips to match block-side lengths after blocks have been quilted in steps 7 and 8 of Assembly.

From backing:

- Cut 9 (10" by fabric width) strips.
  Subcut 36 (10") G squares.

From batting:

- Cut 9 (10" by fabric width) strips.
  Subcut 36 (10") squares.

Chris Suggests

Use scraps to cut the 10" backing and batting squares. Just be sure the batting scraps are all of similar fiber content and loft.

Assembly

1. Draw a diagonal line from corner to corner on the wrong side of each B square.

2. Select four same color family A squares. Position and stitch a B square to a corner of each A square along the marked lines (Figure 1). Trim seam allowances to ¼". Press the seams of two of the pieced squares toward B and two toward A.

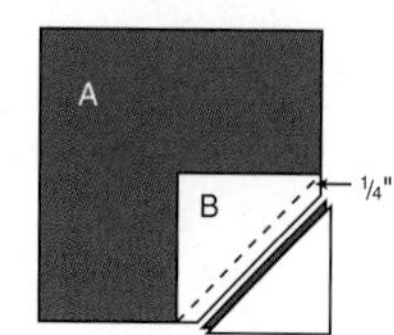

Figure 1

3. Arrange the four squares into two rows of two squares each, with the B corners in the center (Figure 2). Press corner seams in opposite directions.

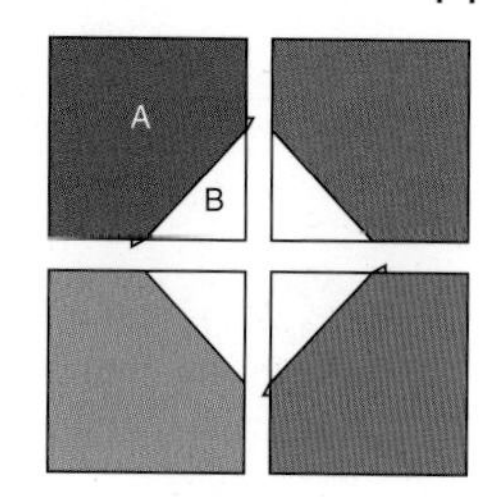

Figure 2

4. Stitch the squares together in rows and the rows together to form a 10" pieced square; press all seams open.

5. Repeat steps 2–4 to make a total of 36 Paint Box blocks.

6. Layer G, right side down, with a batting square and one pieced block, right side up and centered (Figure 3); pin-baste to secure. Repeat with remaining backing and batting squares and blocks.

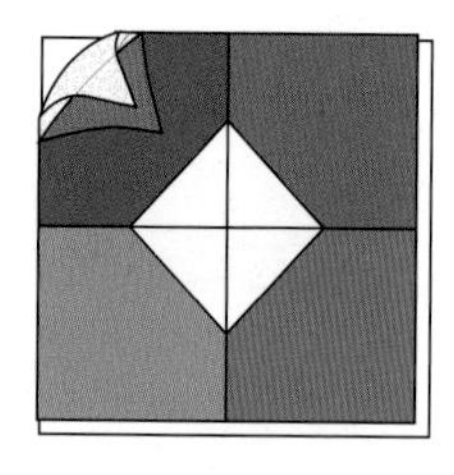

Figure 3

7. Quilt blocks as desired. ***Note:*** *Sample is machine-quilted with concentric lines around the white center, using matching thread. The white center is hand-quilted with a single echo line ¾" from the seam using pearl cotton in a color to match the block*

8. Trim each square to make 9½" square Paint Box blocks.

Chris Suggests

Remember that if you choose a dense quilting pattern, the block will shrink. Measure your blocks and trim them to match the smallest block measurement.

9. Arrange blocks into six rows of six blocks each. Label each block with a row and placement designation as shown in Figure 4.

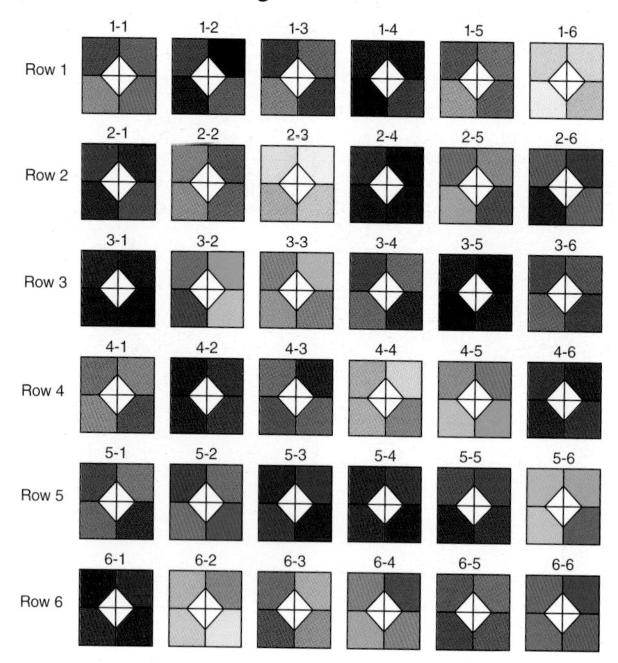

Figure 4

10. Fold and press the C strips in half lengthwise, wrong sides together.

11. Attach an even-feed or walking foot to machine for remainder of construction.

12. Position and pin a C strip on the backing side of block 1-1 along the edge that will be adjacent with block 1-2, raw edges even and referring to Figure 5.

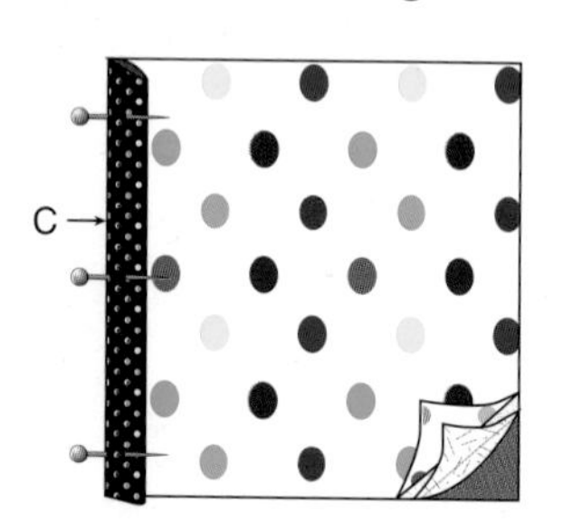

Figure 5

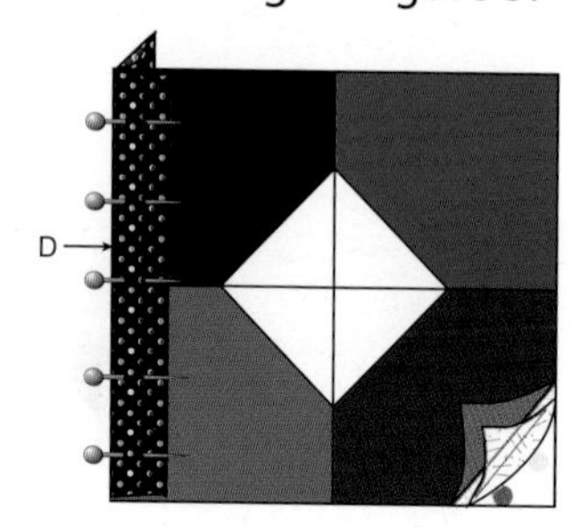

Figure 6

13. Position a D strip along the same edge as C on the right side of block 1-1, right sides together, and pin through all layers referring to Figure 6.

14. Stitch through all layers using a ¼" seam allowance.

15. To attach block 1-2, pin side adjacent to block 1-1 to raw edge of D keeping C free; stitch using a ¼" seam allowance (Figure 7).

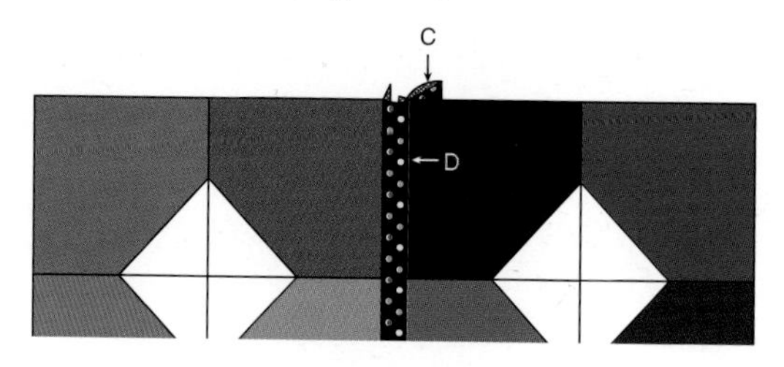

Figure 7

16. Turn the blocks backing side up and press C over the seam area covering both stitching lines. Hand-stitch the folded edge to the backing using a slipstitch (Figure 8).

Figure 8

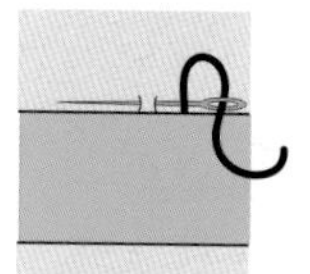

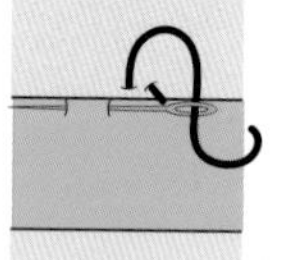

Slipstitch

17. Repeat to join blocks in six rows of six blocks each as arranged.

18. Measure the row lengths when completed and trim the E and F strips to match if necessary. Join rows in the same manner as blocks using E strips on the backing side and F strips on quilt top. Match block sashing strips row to row, creating a straight line vertically referring to the Placement Diagram.

19. Refer to Quilt-As-You-Go String Pieced Blocks on page 6 for more detail on joining and binding blocks and rows.

20. Bind quilt using 2¼" strips to complete quilt. ■

"This quilt reminds me of the excitement I felt as a child each time I got a brand-new paint box—before my enthusiasm resulted in all of the squares being a different shade of brown because I couldn't take the time to clean my brush!" —Chris Malone

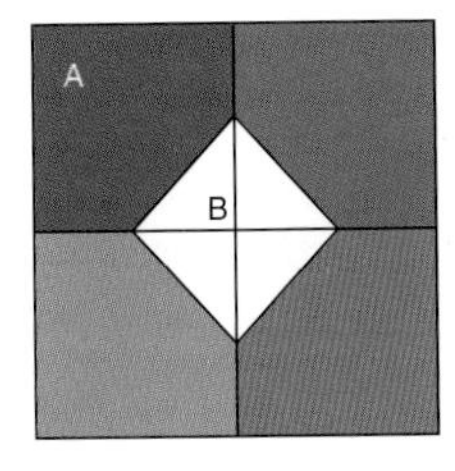

Paint Box
9" x 9" Finished Block
Make 36

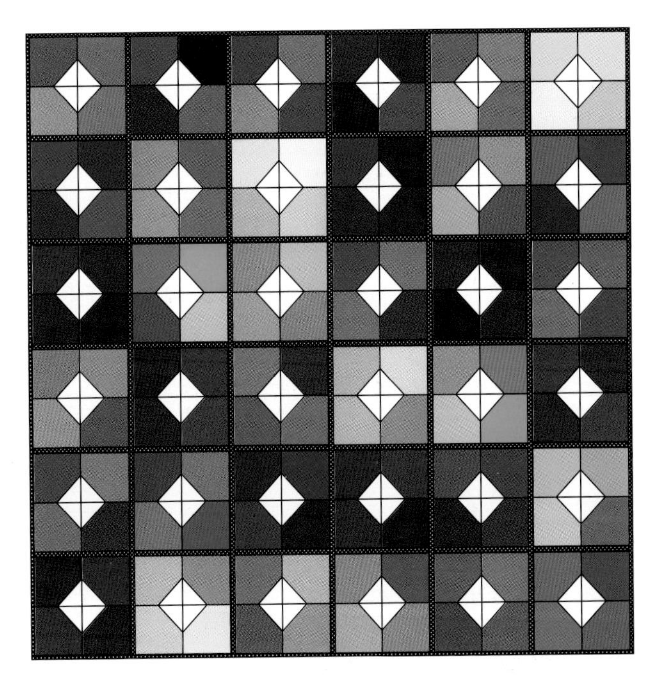

Paint Box Squares
Placement Diagram 57½" x 57½"

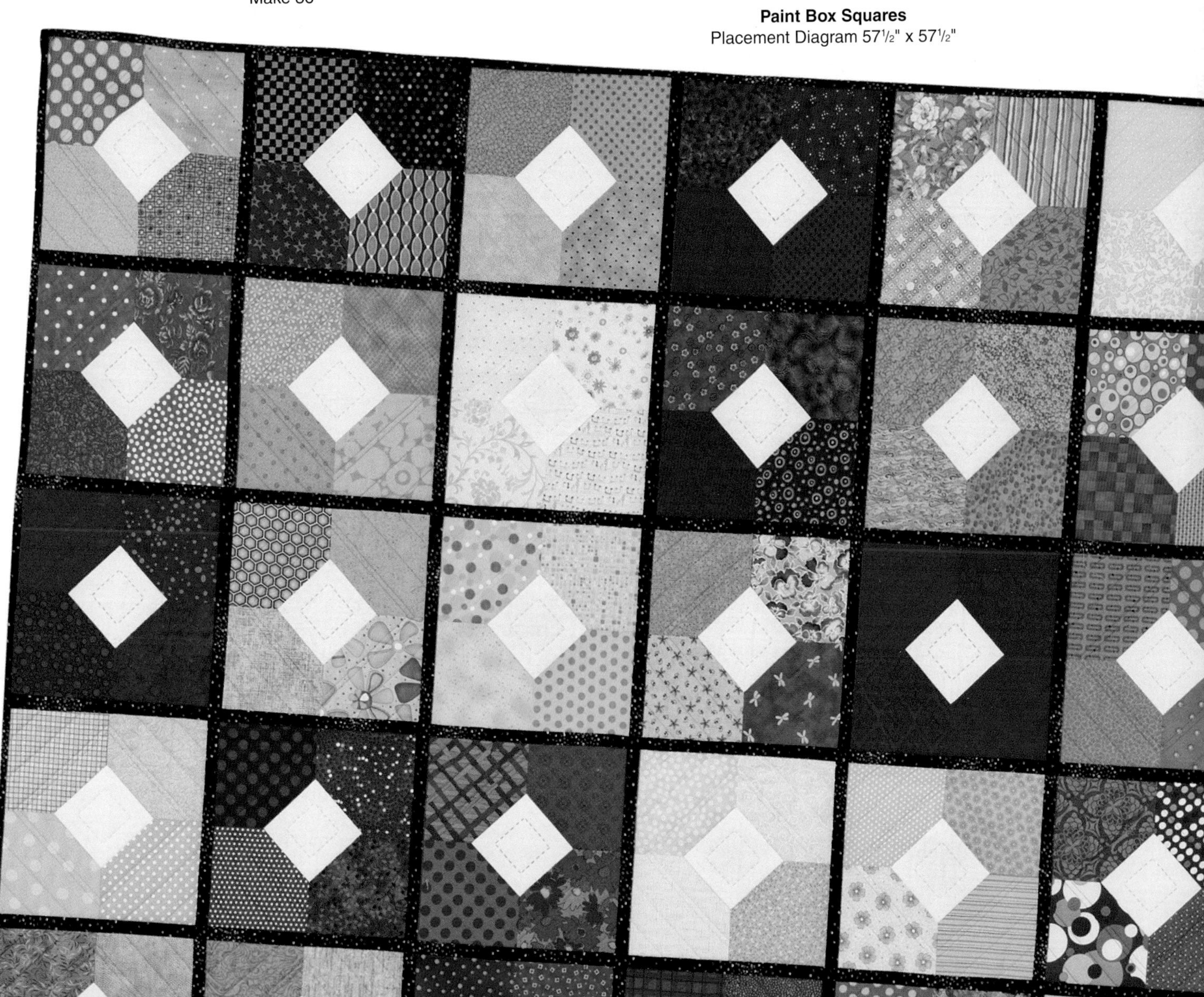

Stained Glass Zigzag

Design by Holly Daniels

Just think of all the fun color options for this project. Use a stitch-and-flip technique to create the blocks and then simply attach the black sashing, and you will have a gorgeous quilt that looks like stained glass windows, not to mention it's reversible!

Specifications

Skill Level: Intermediate
Quilt Size: 52" x 62"
Block Size: 6" x 18" finished
Number of Blocks: 21

Materials

- 1⅛ yard each yellow, red and orange tonals
- 2¾ yards backing
- 3 yards black solid
- Batting 60" x 70"
- Thread
- 6½" square ruler
- Point trimming ruler (optional)
- Basic sewing tools and supplies

Cutting

From yellow tonal:

- Cut 3 (4¾" by fabric width) strips.
  Subcut 21 (4¾") A squares.
- Cut 6 (2½" by fabric width) G/H border strips.

From red tonal:

- Cut 3 (3⅞" by fabric width) strips.
  Subcut 22 (3⅞") squares. Cut each square on one diagonal to make 44 D triangles.
- Cut 2 (6½" by fabric width) strips.
  Subcut 22 (3½" x 6½") E rectangles.

From orange tonal:

- Cut 2 (3⅞" by fabric width) strips.
  Subcut 20 (3⅞") squares. Cut each square on one diagonal to make 40 D triangles.
- Cut 2 (6½" by fabric width) strips.
  Subcut 20 (3½" x 6½") E rectangles.

From backing:

- Cut 4 (19" by fabric width) strips.
  Subcut 21 (7" x 19") block base rectangles.
- Cut 6 (2½" by fabric width) H/G border strips.

From solid black:

- Cut 5 (3⅞" by fabric width) strips.
  Subcut 42 (3⅞") squares. Cut each square on 1 diagonal to make 84 B triangles.
- Cut 3 (7¼" by fabric width) strips.
  Subcut 11 (7¼") squares. Cut each square on both diagonals to make 44 C triangles. Discard 2.
- Cut 18 (1½" by fabric width) strips.
  Subcut 36 (1½" x 18½") F connecting and binding strips.
- Cut 6 (1½" by fabric width) I connecting and binding strips.
- Cut 11 (1½" by fabric width) J/K connecting and binding strips.

From batting:

- Cut 21 (7" x 19") rectangles.
- Cut 2 (2½" x 56½") G and 2 (2½" x 50½") H border strips.

Assembly

Use a scant ¼" seam allowance and stitch right sides together unless otherwise indicated.

Completing the Blocks

1. Referring to Figure 1, mark a 3"-square grid centered on each piece of 7" x 19" batting.

2. Layer batting rectangles, marked side up, on the wrong side of 7" x 19" backing rectangles and pin to create a block base. ***Note:*** *Block base is larger than finished block size.*

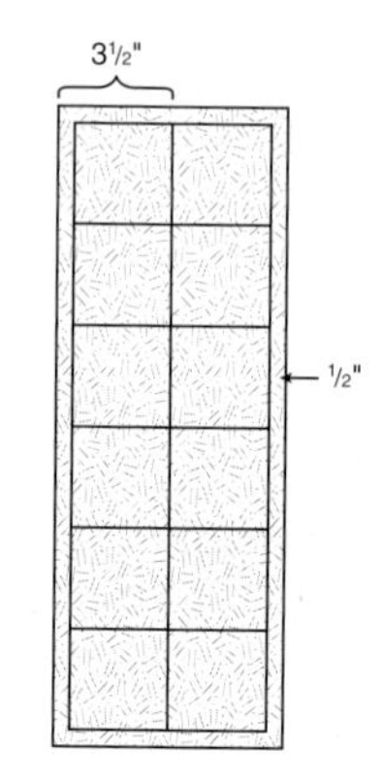

Figure 1

3. To make a Red Stained Glass block, position A on block base diagonally, lining up points on marked center grid lines (Figure 2); pin in place.

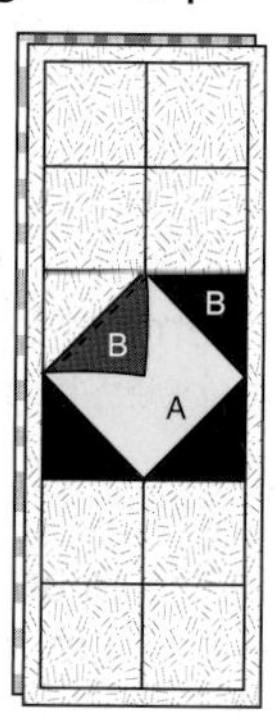

Figure 2

4. Using a scant ¼" seam allowance, stitch a B triangle to one side of A. Flip B away from A and press. Pin to hold. Repeat to add B triangles to all sides of A, creating a square-in-a-square unit referring again to Figure 2.

5. Position C on one end of the square-in-a-square unit using grid lines to center. Stitch, flip and press C away from the square-in-a-square unit; pin. Repeat on opposite end (Figure 3).

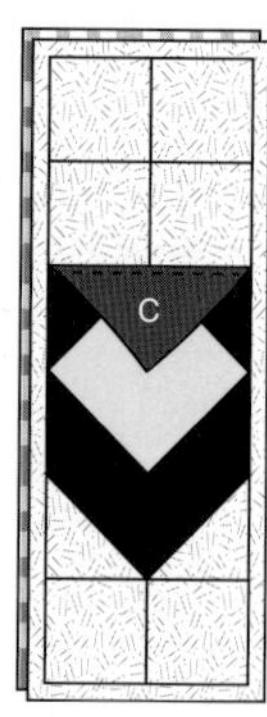

Figure 3

6. Add red D triangles (Figure 4) and E rectangles (Figure 5) to the block base in the same manner using the marked grid to keep pieces centered.

Figure 4

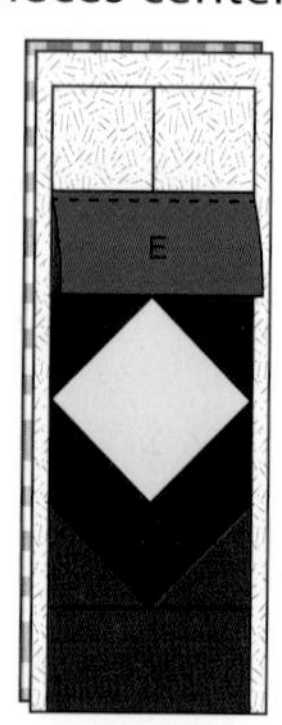

Figure 5

7. Quilt block as desired.

8. Square and trim block to 6½" x 18½". ***Note:*** *For best accuracy, measure 9¼" from center of A to ends of block and 3¼" from center of A on each side.*

9. Repeat steps 3–8 to make 11 Red Stained Glass blocks and 10 Orange Stained Glass blocks.

10. Referring to the Placement Diagram, arrange blocks in three rows of seven blocks.

Connecting & Binding the Blocks

1. Referring to Figure 6, stitch an F strip to adjacent long sides of first two blocks in first block row. Press strips away from blocks.

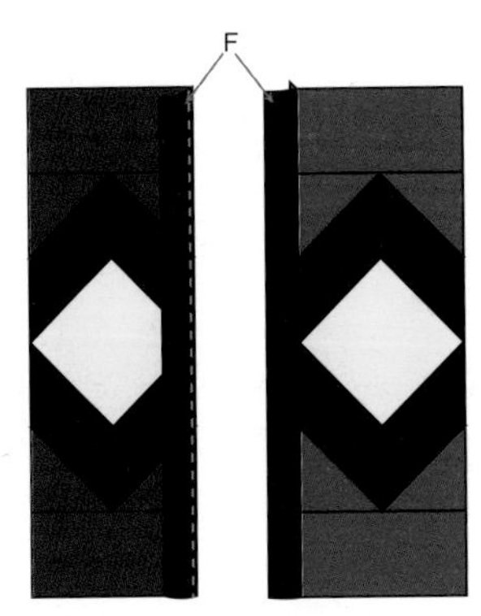

Figure 6

2. With quilt top sides together, match the F seam allowances and pin. Stitch the F pieces together next to the raw edge of the previously stitched seam as shown in Figure 7.

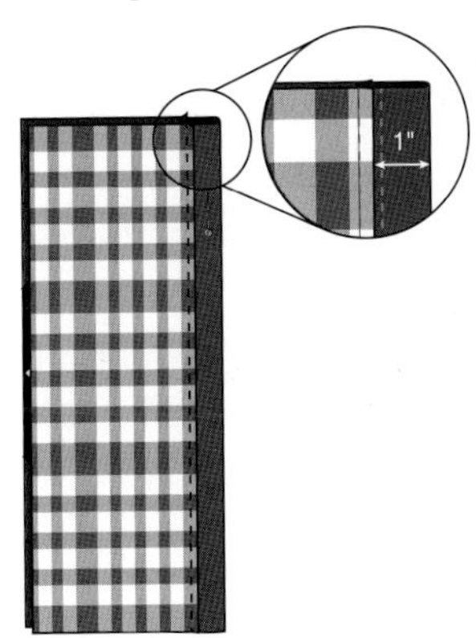

Figure 7

3. Fold raw edge of F to wrong side once and press. Lay blocks quilt top side down on ironing board and fold each F strip over seam allowances as shown in Figure 8. ***Note:*** *Folded edge of F should cover the seams, referring again to Figure 8.*

Figure 8

4. Whipstitch folded edge of F to backing to complete connecting and binding the seam allowance (Figure 9).

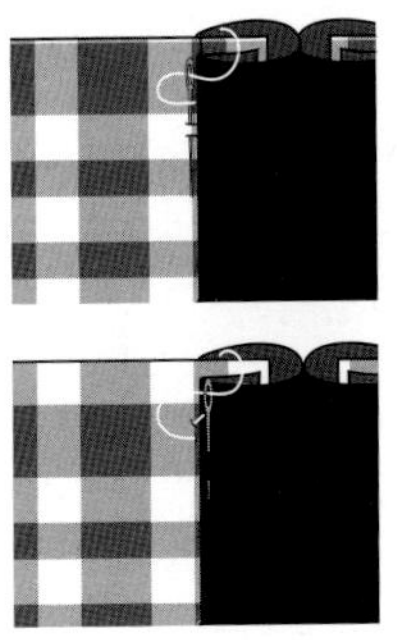

Figure 9

5. Repeat steps 1–4 connecting and binding blocks in pairs across the row, and then connecting and binding the block pairs to complete the block row. Repeat to make three rows as arranged.

Connecting & Binding the Rows

1. Stitch black I strips together on short ends with a straight seam to make one long strip; press seams open. Subcut into four 1½" x 46½" I strips

2. Stitch I strips to bottom of first row and top of second row; trim to match row width if necessary. Repeat steps 1–4 of Connecting & Binding the Blocks to connect and bind first and second rows, matching block corners.

3. Repeat the connecting and binding steps to connect the bottom of the second row to the top of the third block row to complete the quilt center.

Adding Borders & Completing the Quilt

1. Stitch yellow tonal G/H strips together on short ends to make one long strip; press seams open. Repeat with backing G/H strips.

2. Cut the long yellow tonal strip into two each 2½" x 56½" G side borders and 2½" x 50½" H top and bottom borders. Repeat with long backing strip to cut matching back borders.

3. Stitch J/K strips together to make one long strip. Cut four each 1½" x 56½" J and 1½" x 50½" K connecting and binding strips.

4. Layer backing G, right side down, batting G and yellow tonal G, right side up. Baste ⅛" from both long edges or quilt as desired.

5. Refer to steps 1–4 of Connecting & Binding the Blocks to connect and bind the layered G border to one side of the quilt center using J connecting and binding strips.

6. Repeat steps 4 and 5 to add another layered G border to the opposite side of the quilt top and layered H borders with K, connecting and binding strips to the top and bottom.

7. Bind quilt using 2½"-wide binding strips to complete the quilt. ■

Holly Suggests

This is not a hard block to piece, but if you are careless in your piecing, you will end up with crooked, wobbly blocks. Mark the batting as suggested so that you have landmarks to look for—especially at the center top of the block—and piecing will become much neater.

Orange Stained Glass Block
6" x 18" Finished Block
Make 10

Red Stained Glass Block
6" x 18" Finished Block
Make 11

Stained Glass ZigZag
Placement Diagram 52" x 62"

Strippy Table Set

Designed & Quilted by Julie Weaver

Here's a project you can complete in a day. It's a simple sew-and-flip set that has the option to add appliqué.

Specifications

Skill Level: Beginner
Place Mat Size: 18" x 12"
Table Runner Size: 42" x 15"

Materials

Materials are for two place mats and one table runner with appliqué embellishments.

- Scraps brown print
- 36 (1½" x 15") strips total in variety of tan, beige and cream prints
- 42 (1½" x 18") strips total in variety of tan, beige and cream prints
- 1 fat quarter each of green prints 1 and 2
- ⅞ yard green print 3
- 2⅓ yards backing
- 2⅓ yards 45"-wide batting
- Thread
- 1½ yards paper-backed fusible web
- Fabric-basting spray (optional)
- Even-feed or walking presser foot
- Basic sewing tools and supplies

Julie Suggests

Besides being fast and easy, this project is great for scraps! You can use it with any themed appliqué, and it looks great. And it is easy to enlarge or reduce—just add or delete strips for a new size.

Cutting

From green print 3:

- Cut 6 (2½" by fabric width) strips for binding.
  Set aside remainder for appliqué.

From backing:

- Cut 1 (18" by fabric length) strip.
  Subcut 1 (18" x 50") rectangle for table runner.
- Cut 1 (15" by fabric length) strip.
  Subcut 2 (15" x 24") rectangles for place mats.

From batting:

- Cut 1 (18" by fabric length) strip.
  Subcut 1 (18" x 50") rectangle for table runner.
- Cut 1 (15" by fabric length) strip.
  Subcut 2 (15" x 24") rectangles for place mats.

Completing the Place Mats

1. Position and smooth a 15" x 24" batting rectangle on wrong side of same-size backing rectangle.

2. Select one 1½" x 15" tan, beige or cream strip and position, wrong side down, 1" from one short end of layered rectangles on batting side (Figure 1).

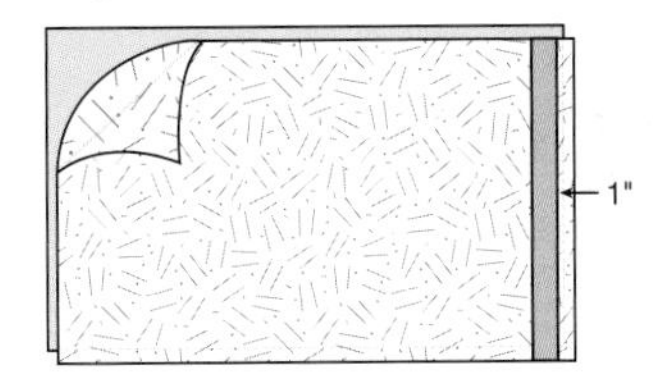

Figure 1

3. Layer a second 1½" x 15" strip on the first strip right sides together, matching edges; stitch along one long edge using a ¼" seam allowance and referring to Figure 2.

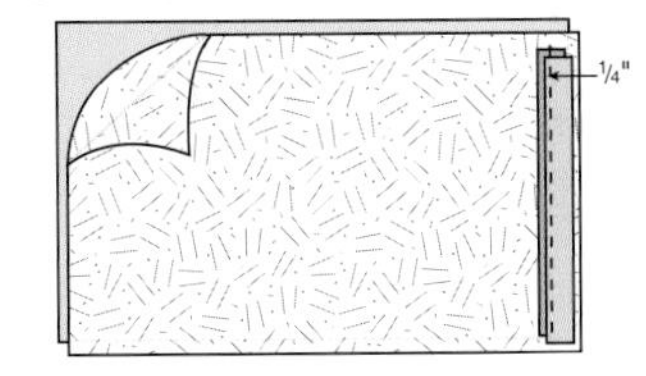

Figure 2

Julie Suggests

Use your walking foot for these projects. You can sew on the strips and binding, as well as stitching the appliqués with a blanket stitch, without having to worry about puckering.

4. Press second strip away from first strip (Figure 3).

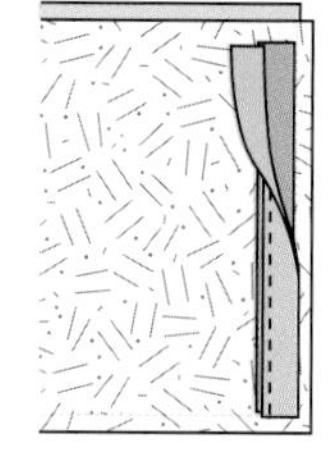

Figure 3

Julie Suggests

Be sure to press, press, press the strips as you sew, and press the backing. Keep everything nice and flat.

5. Repeat steps 2–4 to stitch and flip 18 (1½" x 15") tan, beige or cream strips to the batting/backing rectangle to make a place mat base as shown in Figure 4. Baste loose long edges of first and last strips to base.

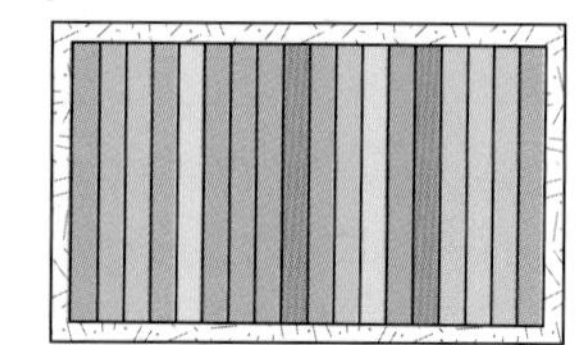

Figure 4

6. Position ruler and trim a long edge of the place mat base, straightening the strip edges referring to Figure 5a.

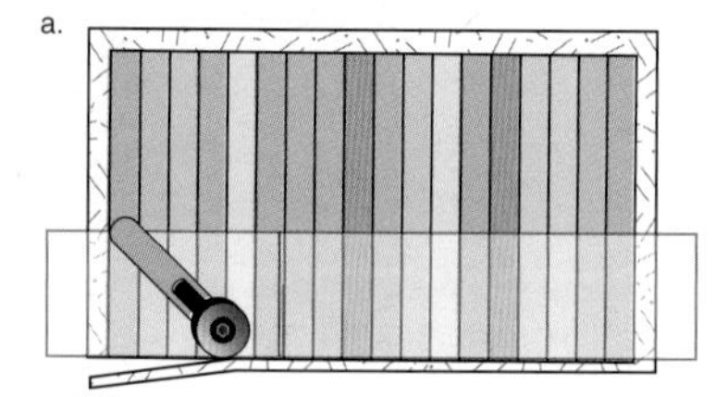

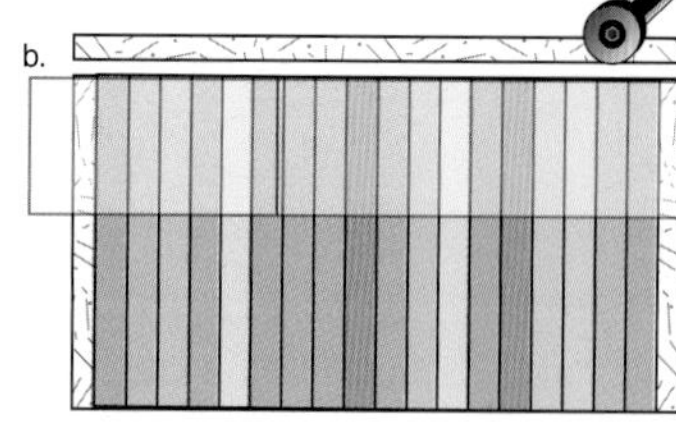

Figure 5

7. Measure 12" from the straightened edge and trim the opposite long side of the place mat base (Figure 5b).

8. Trim batting and backing even with strips on short edges.

9. Using patterns provided on pattern insert, cut a large tree from one of the green prints as desired and a large trunk from brown print scrap. Apply trunk and tree appliqués to place mat referring to Placement Diagram for placement and Raw-Edge Fusible Appliqué on page 17.

10. Prepare binding from two binding strips and bind place mat edges.

11. Repeat all steps to make a second place mat.

Completing th

1. Position anc
on wrong side c

2. Repeat steps 2–
add 42 (1½" x 18") ta
the batting/backing l

3. Repeat steps 6–8 of C
straightening and trimmin
runner to 15" x 42".

4. Using patterns provided on pat
two large and four small trees from gree
desired; cut two large and four small trunks from brown print scraps. Apply tree appliqués to runner referring to Placement Diagram for placement and Raw-Edge Fusible Appliqué on page 17.

5. Prepare binding from remaining binding strips and bind edges to complete the table runner. ■

"So many times we, as quilters, would like to give a gift that we've made but don't have anything "just right" on hand. This set can be started and finished in one day and lends itself to just about everything—think Christmas, Thanksgiving, Easter, spring, summer, winter, fall, birthday, etc." —Julie Weaver

Strippy Table Place Mat
Placement Diagram 18" x 12"

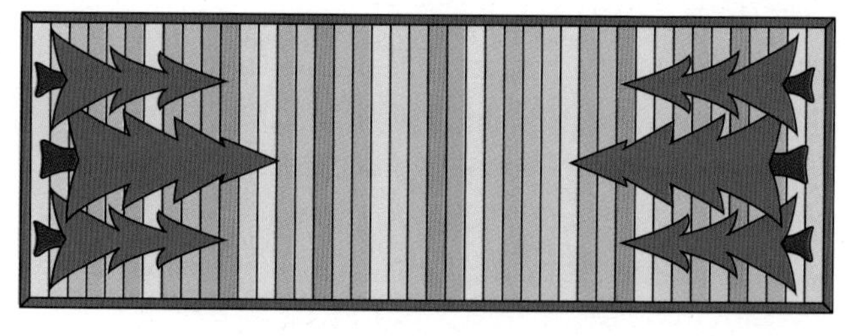

Strippy Table Set Table Runner
Placement Diagram 42" x 15"

Gina Gempesaw
Code of Love Bed Runner, page 3

Ann Lauer
Dine O Mite, page 26

Chris Malone
Paint Box Squares, page 35

Nancy Vasilchik
Charming Puffy Crib Quilt, page 18

Julie Weaver
Strippy Table Set, page 45

Carol Zentgraf
Crazy Blocks Quilt, page 9

Project Gallery

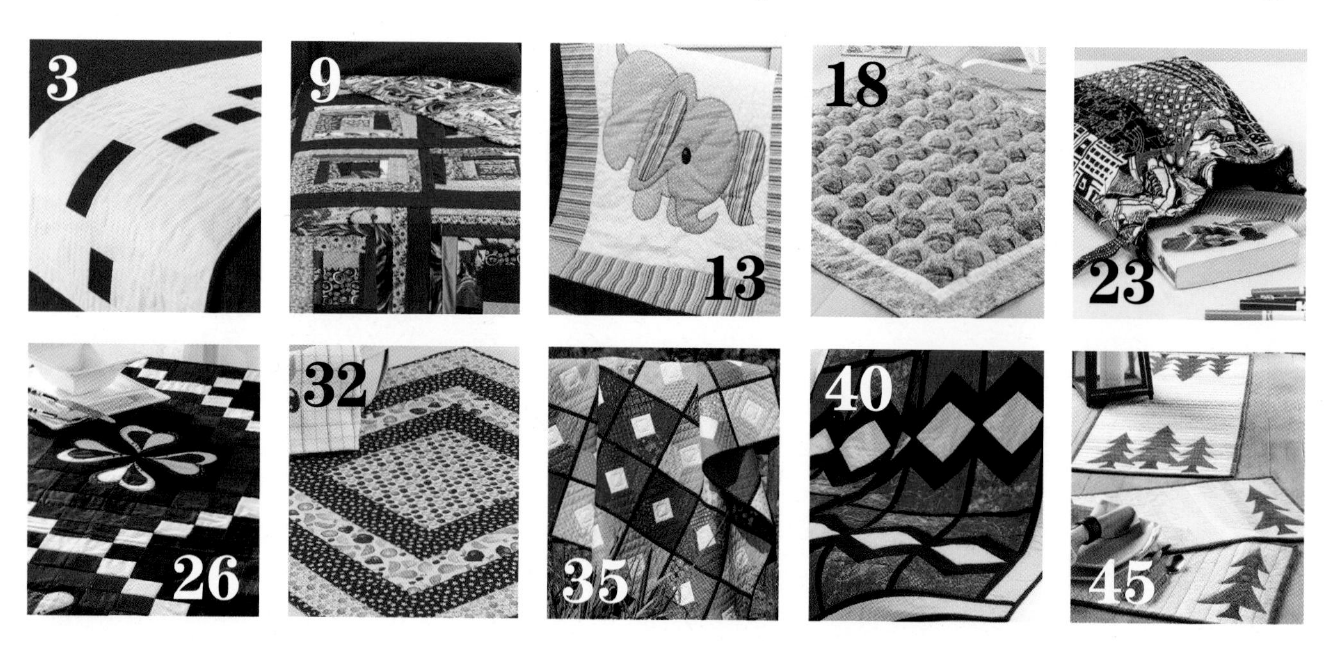

Annie's® *Quilt It As You Go* is published by Annie's, 306 East Parr Road, Berne, IN 46711. Printed in USA.

RETAIL STORES: If you would like to carry this pattern book or any other Annie's publication, visit AnniesWSL.com.

Every effort has been made to ensure that the instructions in this pattern book are complete and accurate. We cannot, however, take responsibility for human error, typographical mistakes or variations in individual work. Please visit AnniesCustomerCare.com to check for pattern updates.

ISBN: 978-1-59635-670-2
5 6 7 8 9

Five Geneseo Monuments

Exhibition Catalog

BRIDGE GALLERY

December 4, 2019

Exhibit Curators: *Rachel Balfoort, Elana Everden,*
Olivia Delahunt, Ryan Brock
Juliana Kuryla, Rachel Mihlstin
Thomas Mossey, Jacob Overshire
Jessica Pisano, Ireland Scanlon
Olivia Schoenfeld, Mercedes Simpson
Kayla Whalen

Acknowledgements

The museum studies class would like to thank James Whitehead, program chair of Association for the Preservation of Geneseo, Judith Hunter, member of the statue of J. S. Wadsworth erection committee, Kurt Cylke, associate professor of sociology, Anna Kowalchuk, director/administrator of the Livingston County Historical Museum, Sally Wood and Liz Porter, members of Livingston County Historial Society Museum board, Amie Alden, Livingston County Historian, Andrew Chanler, Geneseo Fire Chief for helping students with the information about the landmarks and allowing them to learn interview-taking skills. We also would like to express our sincere gratitude to Liz Argentieri, Special Collections/Reference Librarian for helping us with archival material, Allison Brown, Digital Publishing Services Manager for helping with this catalog and Lori Houtz for administrative support.

Contents

The Big Tree

Jessica Pisano, Ryan Brock, Mercedes Simpson

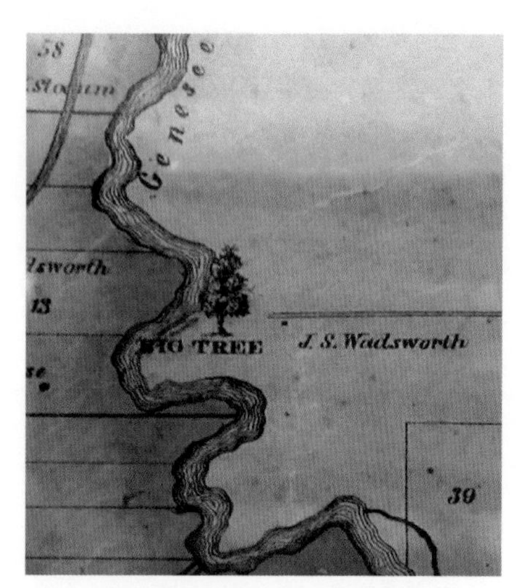

Historical Map found in Livingston County Historical Society Museum

The Big Tree is a unique addition to this collection of landmarks. It was not man made in remembrance, like most of the other things found in this collection. In fact, from it other things were made, and while it lived an ecosystem flourished. Located at the Livingston County Historical Museum, the Big Tree is the five ton remnants of a once very living 300 year old massive oak tree.[1] Aptly named for its size, the historic Big Tree has stood witness to many generations of people and has served as a symbol and relic to very different cultures at very different times. The Big Tree is a prominent symbol of Geneseo and depending on which lens you view it through, can have multiple meanings to different individuals. The Big Tree stood on the east bank of the Genesee River until 1857, when it fell due to rising flood waters, despite efforts to save it. For the Seneca tribe and the larger Haudenosaunee confederacy, it served as a landmark to guide their way and help them identify where they were. The massive appearance of the tree made it easy to identify, therefore making it a natural navigational symbol for the newly arrived colonists. It even appears on official maps, which can also be seen in the Livingston County Historical Society Museum's collection.

The Big Tree is most commonly associated with the Big Tree Treaty, but the name of the Treaty refers to the region, not the actual tree. The council site of the treaty was located near Wadsworth Log Cabin owned by William and James Wadsworth. Robert Morris, a powerful political figure and financier, paid for feasts, beads, and furs in attempts to persuade the Seneca to sell four million acres of their land.[2] The deliberations for the treaty took days and in the end the decision was left to the females of the Seneca group. Seneca females, as part of a democratic government, had more rights than

1 *Up & down the River: Art & Geography of the Genesee River.* Geneseo, NY: Genesee Valley Council on the Arts, 1977.

2 *Up & down the River: Art & Geography of the Genesee River.* Geneseo, NY: Genesee Valley Council on the Arts, 1977.

white female settlers and were included in the deliberations, in the end the deciding vote was left to them. The democratic process observed by the Seneca nation served as inspiration to the Founding Fathers for the structure of The United States Government. Originally these women did not have any interest in selling the land, yet after two weeks of negotiation they decided to sign. A lot of this can be considered directly related to manipulation and power dynamics. For instance, gifts and liquor were used to incentivize the sale. Overall, they had little respect for the majority of the tribe leaders, referring to Red Jacket as "prey to liquor" and Cornplanter as a "half-breed Seneca chief."[3] At the conclusion of negotiations, three million acres of land changed hands at the low price of one hundred thousand dollars.

Chief Cornplanter, Frederick Bartoli, 1796

At the conclusion of the treaty, the Senecas were left with four small reservations of land to host their community, a small portion of what they used to call home. The Seneca could be seen as better off than many other Native American tribes who were forced onto reservations without compensation in completely different states than their original homes. However, it was clear, "For the Senecas it was sunset, but for the young pioneers who soon moved into the land it was a new dawn."[4] This may be why the Big Tree is often called the Wadsworth Oak.

The Big Tree is a polarized symbol shared between the Seneca Nation and white settlers. A hundred years after signing the Big Tree Treaty, members of the Seneca Nation voiced their ill will regarding the deal. Andrew John was recorded exclaiming, "From the standpoint of my race many incidents of the most disgraceful tricks and robberies were perpetrated upon the poor untutored sons of the forest. It would have been strange indeed if the natives had borne tamely such wholesale robbery of their property."[5] In 1997, 200 years post-treaty, the Seneca Nation joined the Livingston County community and erected a commemoration plaque. From the Seneca perspective, the plaque stands today to remember the unfair, dishonorable theft of their land.

3 *Up & down the River: Art & Geography of the Genesee River*. Geneseo, NY: Genesee Valley Council on the Arts, 1977.

4 Dutch VanRy, " Dedicating the Plaque Marking the Council House of the Treaty of Big Tree" (dedication speech, September 14, 1997)

5 Dutch VanRy, " Dedicating the Plaque Marking the Council House of the Treaty of Big Tree" (dedication speech, September 14, 1997)

White settlers held a decidedly opposite view of the Big Tree treaty. The Seneca people were viewed as "savages" that were easily swayed. In fact, settlers provided Native Americans liquor and trinkets to incentivize a successful land transaction. Select historical representations refer to the Big Tree as the Wadsworth Oak. The Wadsworth Estate has a desk made from the Big Tree itself. White settlers took great, perhaps excessive amounts, of pride in the Big Tree treaty and their successful western expansion without considering the detriment caused to the Seneca Nation.

The Big Trcc is important as a symbol of past and present of this community. The Big Tree first serves as a symbol of the Seneca Community that once thrived in the areas of Geneseo. Yet in the same way, it is a symbol of the Native community's oppression that they continue to overcome today. Although the Wadsworths may rightfully be seen as historic heroes, it is important to remember that the Big Tree existed long before they gained their foothold in their new land of the Genesee River Valley and it should not be seen as The Wadsworth Oak. Today's Geneseo community looks to the Big Tree as a symbol of strength and endurance. It is a symbol of the pride in which the people of Geneseo take in their historic past. It serves as a link to that historic past and serves as a reminder of the people who came before them. By preserving The Big Tree and opening their new exhibit that highlights the pre-colonial past of the area the Livingston County Historical Society Museum has helped preserve the past to help teach future generations that there is strength in community.

I ran into Sally and Liz, President and Vice President of the Board of Directors at the Livingston County Historical Society Museum when I went in to photograph the Big Tree exhibit. Sally seemed excited to show me around the exhibit, her enthusiasm was contagious. After allowing me to roam the museum with my camera, Sally showed me a map of the area made in the 1800s that used the Big Tree as a landmark.

As we spoke I remembered reading in a source book that there was a desk commissioned by James Wadsworth out of some of the remnants of the Big Tree after it fell. I asked Sally if she knew anything about the desk. Her eyes lit up and she energetically motioned for me to follow her to the next room. There against the wall was the secretary style desk that was commissioned by James Wadsworth.

Wadsworth desk, made from The Big Tree

Sally and Liz indulged me with one last question before I left. I asked both of them what they

The Big Tree, found in the Livingston County Historical Society Museum

thought the Big Tree meant to the community of Geneseo. Liz Porter said she believed the big tree was a symbol of strength and survival. She also mentioned that she was overwhelmed by the support the community offered when they began fundraising.

She said it took no time at all to raise the needed funds. Sally mentioned the historic value of the Big Tree. She remembered coming to the museum as a child in the fourth grade and seeing the Big Tree. At that time it was housed outside, and apparently looked much larger back then.

Colette Lemmon is the Curator of Exhibitions at the Iroquois Indian Museum in Howes Cave, New York. An important stipulation that Lemmon has made for the purposes of this interview is that she is not Haudenosaunee. She is a Museum Professional who has worked and learned over the span of many years from the Haudenosaunee. The following opinions and thoughts should by no means be considered to hold the weight of authority of the Haudenosaunee community. As it comes to The Big Tree as a symbol, we must remember what this tree meant to the Haudenosaunee themselves. Lemmon describes the traditional values of Haudenosaunee as including respect and care for all the elements that are considered gifts of the natural world. In addition, the importance of considering the impact of one's actions on generations to come. I think this is important to consider as we look at Geneseo through the lens of The Big Tree, it embodies the importance and consideration of the natural world that perfectly align with Haudenosaunee values. As Lemmon states, "Respect for and showing gratitude towards the natural world and its gifts are foundational to traditional Haudenosaunee culture." The Thanksgiving Address, referred to as Ganö:nyök in Seneca, opens and closes all gatherings even today and acknowledges each individually. As Lemmon stresses, on a daily basis members of the Haudenosaunee acknowledge the irreplaceable value of the land, water, medicinal plants, and traditional artistic methods. Individually and through collaborative efforts they protect and preserve their traditional values. As Lemmon states, "If I understand accurately, the current loss of health & deterioration of the natural world is part of Seneca/Haudenosaunee prophecies and considered a warning."

As Lemmon explains, another traditional value of the Haudenosaunee is maintaining sovereignty as a distinct nation/group of nations. The Big Tree as a symbol has association with The Big Tree Treaty that effectively took their lands. The overarching theme of this treaty is colonization. As Lemmon makes clear, colonization affected the Haudenosaunee in countless ways. As she makes clear, "With colonization land use changed; gender roles & responsibilities changed; languages were lost; much indigenous knowledge was lost; Christianity undermines traditional ways of life & thinking; western values and assimilation become a big part of the mix; government structures change from traditional system to elected (in most Haudenosaunee communities); diet sees dramatic change; Native identity becomes a marketable commodity, shared resources vs individual ownership/personal benefit, etc." Colonization had a great effect on the colonized Haudenosaunee. It must be remembered that "The original authority & rights to these lands which they hold as a consequence of having occupied them for several thousands of years before European contact." Not only this land but everything contained within it including The Big Tree was lost. The Haudenosaunee continue to grieve this loss and Lemmon describes their experience as, "The loss of home, loss of places of memory, loss of important natural resources, sorrow and powerlessness of leaders to prevent its happening..." Yet it is important to acknowledge that the Haudenosaunee continue to function as the oldest democracy on Earth. As Lemmon puts it, their first and true allegiance is to their own nations.

The Big Tree, Livingston County Historical Society Museum

The Bear Fountain Monument: A Symbol of Community

Jake Ovenshire, Juliana Kuryla, and Ireland Scanlon

Central view of the bear monument from Center Street.

Communities around the world often have a symbol they look to when imagining a specific place. For the village of Geneseo, New York, that symbol is the infamous Bear Fountain positioned in the center of Main Street. Anyone who has passed through the town can notice the stature of the fountain as a whole and as a landmark within the community social atmosphere. One opinion you typically may hear about the monument concerns its awkward placement in the middle of the road. However, this center

Close up of Emmeline Wadsworth bear monument.

point within the community simultaneously brings people together and gives use to the historical monument within the changing social structures of an ever-changing society. The Bear Fountain monument has been an irreplaceable symbol of the village of Geneseo, New York since its installment in 1888. The town's efforts to maintain constant restoration efforts of the fountain has survived the changing times of the town.

Herbert Wadsworth and his brother William Austin Wadsworth commissioned the bronze bear to the town in memorial of their mother Emmeline. This monument was

View of Main Street, "Horses At The Fountain". 1900. Courtesy of John and Liz Porter APOG.

put to physical use as a trough for the town's water source at the end of the 17th century in addition to leaving a historical landmark to the town for generations to come. The architect chosen by the Wadsworth brothers held personal ties with their late mother Emmeline. Emmeline had a passion for animals which inspired the brothers when searching to create this monument. Thinking back on a family trip to Switzerland is where the connection lies within the sculpting for the statue and the architects involved. Although there has been some questioning as to who deserves the full credit of the creation of the bear, there are only a few documents stating names involved with the statue, the title is given to Christophe Fratin and Richard Morris Hunt to the rest of the fountain. On Christophe Fratin, he is an architect from France during the early 19th century, he's credited to creating many bronze works produced in France during this era along with Antoine Bayre who was also thought to have some credit to the bear statue ending in no connection at all. As Fratin travels through Europe, he frequents in Switzerland gaining most of his fountain experience from the Swiss seeing as fountains are the main form of art throughout the country. The Wadsworth family had also enjoyed vacationing there, especially the mother Emmeline, which is why the brothers chose Fratin to cast the bronze bear memorial. For the remainder of the fountain, the architect responsible for constructing the monument is Richard Morris Hunt who was a prominent architect of his time. He was involved in creating multiple famous American monuments, in addition to the fountain Hunt also worked with creating the Statue of Liberty as well as the U.S Capitol building. The fact that the Wadsworth were able to get into contact with Hunt to create this piece for the town is in and of itself a monument, it truly shows the stature the Wadsworth family held over the county and surrounding areas. This gives way for a greater historical background context for the town of Geneseo. Combined with the Swiss aspects of the bear at the top of the fountain, and the American architecture of the fountain used with American based marble to create the original bowl for the statue based out of Bradford, Connecticut. The creation of this dedication in full became a whole community event especially once installation took place in the late 19th century, and remained a staple centerpiece within the community since the production, maintaining its place within the community as a gathering place for all who visit or abide within Geneseo.

Hind view of the Bear Fountain circa 1890.

Countless instances have transpired that illustrate the importance and significance of the Bear Fountain as a symbol for the village of Geneseo. The most recognized force that has highlighted the importance of the fountain is the Association for the Preservation of Geneseo. Also known as APOG, this organization has been at the forefront of the Bear Fountains preservation and renovation of the fountain as early as the 1970's when the fountain was riddled with multiple street signs and a traffic light, making the fountain an eyesore to the community. Paul Malo, a Syracuse architect retained by the Association for the Preservation of Geneseo, suggested that the signs and fixtures be moved from the base of the fountain and moved to the street corners, where they still reside today. At one point the complete bottom half of the fountain was hidden by the signs and fixtures. This set into motion a fountain project would be consistent with board policy to "strengthen Main Street, the social and commercial center of the community" budgets costing around 2800 alongside the fountain. This communal involvement can also be attributed to one of SUNY Geneseo's professors, Kurt Cylke, who got involved with APOG in 1997 to replace to terrible looking lanterns that was once held by the famous bear with a more authentic gothic-inspired lantern and 3D images made for the fountain to keep any renovations to the fountain as authentic to the original as possible. His experience can be better understood in the interview that we conducted. As per Malos and Cylke's example, we can see that the fountain as a symbol of Geneseo is powerful enough to evoke strong opinions from the community based on how it's displayed. A more recent instance that illustrated the fountain's importance to the village was when the fountain was struck by a milk truck in 2016, leaving the fountain damaged beyond repair. In a Livingston County newspaper called the Genesee Sun, we can see the steps that were taken to rebuild the monument stat-

Central view of Center Street from the Bear Fountain.

Side view of the Bear Statue from Main Street.

ing that "The Association for the Preservation of Geneseo" (APOG) is partnering with Moorland Studios, a nationally renowned outdoor monument restoration group, to restore the fountain. APOG keeps 3D images of the fountain's every detail since its Gothic lamp was restored years ago." While funding the restoration was done "by a 'trust fund' set aside by the community for the bear fountain in case of such accidents and partially by insurance paid by Upstate Niagara Cooperative Inc., who owns the truck." The steps taken to reinstall this monument like 3D image use and even using a trust fund that the community raised illustrates just how important the Bear Fountain is to the community.

In summation, the community of Geneseo has gone to great lengths so that the Bear Fountain remains an everlasting symbol of Geneseo. With the likes of APOG, Kurt Cylke, and generous Geneseo alumni, it appears that the fountain has sufficient financial and communal support to continue lighting up Main Street. As a monument that all residents and students have come in contact with, the Bear Fountain stands as a symbol of the passion the community of Geneseo embodies.

Interview with Kurt Cylke

Oct 22, 2019

During our research, we had the pleasure of conducting an interview of the very knowledgeable Kurt Cylke, a professor of Sociology here at Geneseo. After moving to the town with his family in 1990, he began to take an interest in the bear fountain, which was conveniently a block away from his new residence. Due to its central location between the school and his home, Cylke would walk by the fountain daily on his way to work. The structure is hardly visually avoidable and with time, Cylke became critical of the fountains appearance. His initial complaint concerned the "fucking ugly latern" that had presumably replaced the original following its destruction. This was not the first time people have been dissatisfied with arbitrary additions to the fountain. In the 1930s, a stop light system was installed to the fountain which was followed by street signs being affixed to the base of the structure in the 1960s. Unsurprisingly, these items did nothing to contribute to the fountains artistic intention and were removed in the 70s due to public backlash. Cylke reacted in a similar way when he joined APOG (Association for the Preservation of Geneseo) to advocate for the replacement of the unsightly lantern. The collaboration between Professor Cylke and APOG began with their consultation with Moorland Studios in New Jersey, the company that was tasked with reproducing the lantern. To fund the restoration, Cylke called upon Geneseo alumni to contribute what they wished to finance the project. The accumulated money totaled $30,000, which was more than enough for the $4,000 lantern restoration. With $26,000 at APOGS's disposal, they were able to purchase a 360 degree detail oriented digital scan of the fountain which would be used as a template for future restorations. This left $6,000 for whatever eventual financial burden was created by the fountain.

Mr. Cylke also informed us about a piece of misinformation regarding the materials used for the original fountain. The granite in the base of the fountain was thought to have come from St. George, Nova Scotia. It was confirmed by Cylke that the stone was extracted from a quarry in Bradford, Connecticut. The company that would reconstruct the base from that same granite used in the original was the Rock of Ages, a globally recognized laser cutting company based in Vermont, where they were able to

Side view of the Bear Fountain via Main Street.

utilize the 360 digital scan. The remaining granite from the destroyed fountain was later repurposed into four benches that now line Main Street in Geneseo. Smaller portions of the stone were broken down and sold as pieces of history at the Livingston County Museum.

Cylke addressed a question we had about the particular usage of a bear for the fountain. Architect Richard Morris Hunt apparently spent a great deal of time in Berne, Switzerland. Berne is actually Swiss for 'bear' and the city hosts about 100 municipal fountains topped with bear figurines. The bear was a dedication to their mother, Emmeline Wadsworth, who died in March 21st 1885. When Emmeline visited Berne with her family, she had taken a particular fondness for these fountains making the fountain dedicated to her a thoughtful tribute. In a way, the memorial serves as a memento of the Wadsworth's mother's trip to Switzerland. As for Hunt, Cylke does not even believe that the architect visited Geneseo to survey the land prior to construction. It seems as though his efforts were done from afar. Cykle clears up an important point for us, the fountain and the actual bear statue were pieced together at the same time.

According to Cykle, there have been few acts of vandalism performed on the fountain. Most of the issues the fountain endured were caused by vehicular accidents. The fountain has come down at least five separate times, says Cykle. He explains how it is not really a big deal because of this. Cykle reinforces our thesis of community involvement by detailing multiple activities that take place with the fountain as a centerpiece. Due to its proximity to SUNY Geneseo, the fountain is used as a post for hanging the homecoming banners. The banner, attached to the bear, actually brought the statue down on a y. Activithe statue on a very windy day. In regard to celebrations concerning younger folk, there is an annual Teddy Bear Parade that takes place on Main Street every year. During Halloween, children dress up and parade around the illuminated fountain. During Christmas time, holiday decorations are hung on the fountain as well, drawing even more attention to the towns centerpiece.

The fountain has now taken on a modern use, a directional divider for a traffic circle. The structure sits at a crossroads at the center of a lengthy Main Street and perpendicular Center Street which often funnels cars into the main drag. Cars can use the fountain to turn onto Center Street or Main Street without completely blocking traffic by stalling in front of it then making a turn. This structure alleviates a potential traffic problem while being more attractive than a set of orange traffic cones.

James Samuel Wadsworth Statue

Rachel Balfoort

James Wadsworth's Background

James Samuel Wadsworth was born on October 30th, 1807 and died on May 8th, 1864. He was a Union general known for his wealth, military expertise and politics. Wadsworth was an influential abolitionist and military hero in the nineteenth century that made a difference in the world and brought honor to Geneseo. This influential man lived in a small town in New York called Geneseo. His life is commemorated by the statue in Gettysburg, Pennsylvania made out of bronze in honor of his military service. However, not a lot of people realize that there is a replica of the same statue hidden behind trees in front of the Livingston County Courthouse in Geneseo.

James was an influential figure, even before his military involvement in the Civil War that garnered him a statue in Gettysburg. Wadsworth was the richest man of the North during the nineteenth century. His family owned property that stretched

James S. Wadsowrth Statue. Novemeber 11, 2019.

General James S. Wadsworth Portrait

twenty four miles from Geneseo to Henrietta. Although James had amassed this great amount of land and was extremely wealthy, he used his fortune in order to donate a full shipload of grain to Ireland during the Irish potato famine in 1845 to 1849. This proved that Wadsworth had the ability to give back to others and to assist his community as best he could. Among his fine qualities of being a well known figure in society, he had a fine education that led him to pursue law at prestigious schools, such as Harvard and Yale. When he did not take the bar exam for being a lawyer, he married Mary Craig Wharton in 1834.

Wadsworth's Political Stance

In addition to being an extremely wealthy philanthropist, the General was also extensively involved in New York politics. Originally a member of the free soil Democrats, Wadsworth beleived that slavery should not be allowed to expand to new states and territories during the presidency of Martin Van Buren in 1837 to 1841. James was passionate about preserving the Union and his opposition to slavery. He focused more on anti-Southern politics than against anti-slavery. For instance, he only donated fifty dollars to a slave who was captured in Wisconsin compared to the full boat of grains that Wadsworth donated to the potato famine. It appears that James wanted to fight against proslavery Southerners and beleived they endangered the freedoms and existence of the republic in order to promote slavery.

New York Republicans wanted Wadsworth to run for governor in 1862, yet he did little campaigning. In his writings and speeches he justified the party label of being an abolitionist as a means to preserve the Union and to punish the South. James only held one speech in New York City for his campaign in which he described in full detail how he was not in favor of the anti-slavery cause. He had garnered eleven thousand votes in total during the election but did not win by only a handful of votes. Due to the lack of votes, Wadsworth's party label changed from a Republican to an Abolitionist. James finally recognized Abolitionism as his main cause and saw it as an effective war measure. He stated in his New York City speech that "We have the right, we are bound, moreover, by the solemn obligations of duty, to use this agency [emancipation], so far as we can, to put an end to this struggle, and to save the lives of white men who are perishing by thousands in this country" (Hunter 37). James decided to serve in the army during the Civil War and enlisted in 1863.

Wadsworth as a General

When the war in Gettysburg began, Wadsworth volunteered as a major even though he was already extremely wealthy and would not be paid throughout the course of the war. President Abraham Lincoln admired the General's attention to his troops and how he took care of them. As Lincoln stationed James at the front lines during the first winter of the Civil War. With Wadsworth's strong background in military skills, his politics also gained a new perspective during the course of the war. For example he reflected : "At the beginning of the war, I was hardly a Republican. I thought slavery should be restricted to the ground where it stood, but was opposed to interfacing with it there. I dreaded insurrections, massacres, and violence" (Hunter 33).

When James' political beliefs began to change, he started to employ slaves in his camp and treated them with the respect they deserved. By Wadsworth having the ability to gain the slave's trust, he was able to figure out the size of the Confederate army in order to attack them. Lincoln was so impressed with his achievements that he appointed James as the military governor of the District of Columbia. This made him in charge of slave runaways and returning them back to their owners under the Fugitive Slave Act. The general wanted to keep the slaves who committed no crimes under hisprotection, however, and ordered soldiers to free slaves who were considered "contrabands" in the middle of the night.

Wadsworth was serving various other positions in the army. During the nineteenth century, Mississippi was in the Union's hands. In the spring of 1864, he was back in the combat field at the Battle of the Wilderness. The war could only be described as a very confusing and chaotic situation. In Virginia, the battle's surrounding had underbrush, scrub, and trees. This made it especially hard for the armies to keep in contact with each other to let them know when an enemy force was attacking. James did something that generals typically did not do. He led the charge to attack enemies on a horse, and while he was on the horse, Wadsworth was shot in the head. The General fell behind

Confederate lines where they took him to the hospital to be taken care of. James was then stated to be in a comatose and proceeded to die behind Confederate lines. Once he passed, Wadsworth was sent back across enemy lines where citizens held ceremonies for James in Rochester and New York City in order to commemorate his legacy.

Wadsworth's Recognition in Gettysburg

James has an abundance of plaques, statues, and monuments dedicated to him throughout the nation. In Gettysburg, Pennsylvania specifically, a statue of Major General James S. Wadsworth was commissioned on March 2nd, 1910 and sketched by R. Hinton Perry. The statue was of a bronze James statue leading his troops onward to battle and forming the line to position them for battle. The New York Monuments Commission "authorized and directed to procure and erect on an appropriate site on the battlefield of Gettysburg, in the State of Pennsylvania, a bronze statue of Brevet Major-General James Samuel Wadsworth, deceased, at an expense not to exceed the sum of Ten thousand dollars" (Authority of the State of New York 12). This statue is located on Seminary Ridge, otherwise known as where General Wadsworth's best known exploit as a commander.

Official party at Wadsworth monument dedication, October 6th, 1914.

Recognition in Geneseo

The statue stands proudly in Gettysburg for people to admire and appreciate James' services to our country. However, not many people realize that General Wadsworth who stands proudly in Gettysburg directing his soldiers into battle, grew up in a small town in Western New York called Geneseo. The town of Geneseo decided to commission a replica of the Gettysburg statue in 2006 by Pepsy M. Kettavong in dedication to his life that he led in Geneseo. The statue was created by The committee did not want

James S. Wadsworth Statue in front of the Livingston Courthouse by Daniel Sanderson

children who grew up in Geneseo believing that this was a stagnant town. The committee firmly believed that the courthouse looked bare and thought it was appropriate to put the statue right in the front. The committee believed that putting the statue in front of the courthouse would allow students in school buses to see the statue and know it was Wadsworth. However, the State Office of New York informed the committee that the statue could not be put in front of courthouse only because people would believe that the statue was originally part of the courthouse. Therefore, the statue is tucked away behind trees and made to look not prominent. The town of Geneseo is not even allowed to put lights around statue because it is not "authentic" to the courthouse.

Geneseo community members were able to raise the funds for the statue since the committee pitched how General Wadsworth was the most prominent Civil War historian that lived right in Geneseo. The committee continued to raise funds for the statue by hosting a lecture about James at the Hartford House in early 2001. The committee also raised the funds through various projects such as a house tour, a two hundred year old birthday party for the General, and appealing to people one on one. The committee also sold T-shirts with a photo of the original artist's model on the shirt. The statue was an exceptionally important community project and was a huge commitment.

Interview with Judith Hunter

Judith Hunter was a former History professor for SUNY Geneseo. She also specialized as a trainee Civil War historian in the 1990s. I met with her on October 10th,

2019 to talk about her process with commissioning the James Samuel Wadsworth Statue by the Livingston County Museum. She stated that James was the richest man of the North during his period. Wadsworth's family-owned property that went from Geneseo to Henrietta. James was involved in New York politics, as at the time he was more anti-Southern politics than anti-slavery. Wadsworth was the first General stationed at the front lines in the first winter of the Gettysburg war. The General conducted interviews of runaway slaves that crossed Union lines and knew where the enemies were located. He ran for governor in the fall of 1862. He had 11,000 votes, but did not win the election. When he loses the election, he serves in the army when Gettysburg wins. In the spring of 1864, Wadsworth was back at the Battle of Wilderness where it was a very confusing and chaotic situation. The war had an abundance of underbrush, scrub, trees, and it was hard for the armies to keep in contact with each other. Judith made it clear that it was atypical of a general to lead a charge on a horse and he was shot in the head because of his bravery. Where the General fell behind Confederate lines, they took him to a hospital where he passed.

Judith visited Gettysburg, Pennsylvania where she saw the James S. Wadsworth statue several times. Yet, it was not until after she taught in Geneseo that she realized the importance of statues and monuments in the fact that they are located everywhere and are apart of history. Hunter thought of James' heroic contribution to the Gettysburg Battle and how there is no monument to him in Geneseo where he grew up. Judith pointed out that while there is the Wadsworth Library located on Second Street in Geneseo, there is nothing to commemorate James S. Wadsworth in particular. Hunter believed that this was out of modesty since many statues and plaques have been dedicated to him throughout the nation. Judith decided that a monument needed to be built here in Geneseo to commemorate his life.

The fundraising process for commissioning the monument was taken upon the community members of Geneseo. They were the ones who helped raise money for the campaign because Wadsworth was the most prominent civil war historian in Geneseo. To raise the funding, the committee hosted a lecture on him and hosted a reception at the Hartford House in early 2001. The committee also raised the money through various projects such as a house tour of the Hartford House, a two-hundred-year-old birthday party for Wadsworth, and appealing to people one on one. Unexpectedly, the statue cost was much less than it was expected so it was easier to commission it sooner. Judith firmly believes that the monument was a very important community project and commitment.

Some particulars of commissioning the statue included the significance of the pose of General Wadsworth. The reason why James is pointing onwards to show that he is directing his troops and forming the line to position them for battle. Another factor was why the statue was commissioned in front of the courthouse. The reason being was that the committee didn't want kids to grow up here thinking that nothing happens around Geneseo. This is also where school buses go by, and children would see the statue when they were going to school. However, the committee ended up being disappointed in the end. The State Office told the committee that the monument could not be put in front of the courthouse since it was not original. Therefore, the statue is tucked away much more and is not prominently in front of the courthouse.

Overall, the biggest takeaway that Hunter would like to see from my exhibit is that the Yankees need to remember the Civil War and what James S. Wadsworth stood for.

Conclusion

General James S, Wadsworth was a man who had sacrificed himself for the right cause of protecting his troops and becoming an abolitionist. This is what we as 21st century citizens should remember James as. He not only affected the world, but brought a significant honor to Geneseo. Although it is located in the most unfortunate spot, it resembles the man that he is and how he brought great honor to a small town in Western New York.

References

Authority of the State of New York, Under the Supervision of the New York Monuments Commission. *Major-General James S. Wadsworth at Gettysburg and Other Fields.* Albany. J.B. Lyon Company, Printers. 1916. Book.

Hunter, Judith. *Abolitionism as Logical Conclusion: General James S. Wadsworth as a Case Study in Anti-Southern Sentiment and the Radicalizing Experience of the Civil War by: Judith A. Hunter.* Charlottesville and London. University of Virginia Press. 2011. Article.

Progression Toward Modernity: Geneseo's Suffragists, The Shaw Sisters

Elana Evenden, Tom Mossey, Kayla Whalen

"And Eventually...They Voted"

In the sweeping world of the Progressive Era, two women grew up to change Geneseo's history and influence future generations. Nicolas and Eleanor Shaw would become the front runners of the Livingston County Suffrage and Temperance movements by inspiring public opinion during town meetings. They took the torch from women like Elizabeth Cady Stanton (1815-1902) and Susan B. Anthony (1820-1906), who passed away around the turn of the century. The Shaw sisters lived in an era where their progressive ideals could be disseminated with the help of the railroad. With the railroad and their progressive ideals, these women were able to see modernity when in 1919 Women's Suffrage was passed in New York. They were products of the moment

Women Fighting for Suffrage During the Progressive Era

Nicholas Shaw, 1913

Eleanor Shaw Smith, 1914

and movements they were living through. The fought for educated, lectured, inspired, empowered women throughout Western New York, and eventually...they voted.

Social and political reforms were the hallmark of the Zeitgeist for the turn of the century in America. From the 1890s up until after the First World War, people began to question the corruption and the problems associated with the modernization of the United States. The women's suffrage movement officially started in 1848 when the First Woman's Rights Convention was held in Seneca Falls, NY, only fifty-five miles from Geneseo. For the first time in history, women were standing up to fight, lobby, and educate the public on matters that truly concerned their sex and their rights. Due to complications both politically and socially, the movement would not gain full traction until the turn of the twentieth century. Urbanization and industrialization had taken its toll on American society, and out of this sprang the final push that the women's suffrage movement needed for the vote. With all of the reforms, women were able to get their voices heard on issues that plagued the women's sphere such as suffrage and temperance, both topics that interested the Shaw Sisters and would become apart of their legacy.

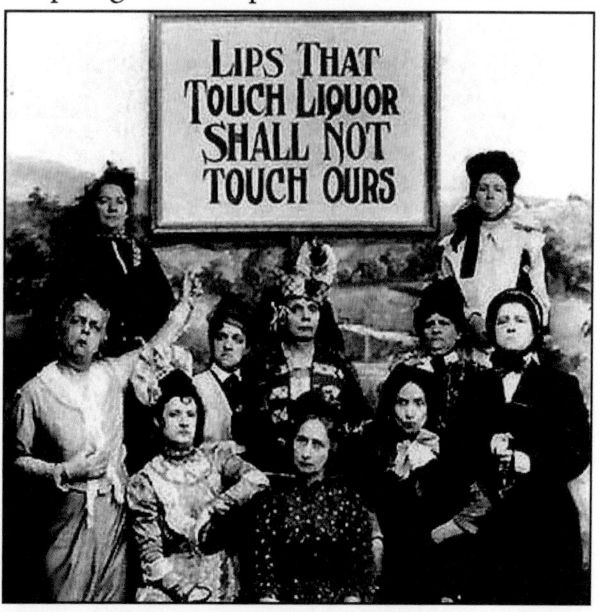

Women Fighting for Temperance, 1800s

In addition to suffrage, the other biggest cause for women at this time was temperance. The Temperance Movement was a reaction against the sales and consumption of alcohol. The movement instituted in 1874 when the Women's Christian Temperance Union (WCTU) was formed. Their main action was to outlaw alcohol for safety concerns, but ultimately for the safety of the family unit.

Although these two movements stayed separate because neither group wanted to delude the other, many women stood for both causes. For example, Nicolas Shaw was very involved in the Women's Suffrage Movement while her sister Eleanor was more involved with the Temperance Movement. In fact, Eleanor was the president of the Livingston County chapter of the WCTU, while Nicolas was not an officer but still sat as a member of the chapter. These causes were both about protecting the feminine sphere. From suffrage giving them political independence and a say in the family dynamic to protection from the harsh realities of alcoholism, women were finally able to fight for the rights they deserved.

Anna Howard Shaw, Aunt to Nicholas and Eleanor

Eleanor and Nicholas were influenced by their aunt, also a feminist, Anna Howard Shaw, was the guiding influence for her nieces' progressive ideas. She has been a prominent figure when the sisters were growing up, and this is why when asked to live with her, Nicolas agreed. She had also been contemporaries with the Suffrage movement's founding mothers such as Elizabeth Cady Stanton, who presented at the First Woman's Rights Convention in 1848 and Susan B. Anthony, who was arrested for voting in 1872. Howard Shaw was a leading figure within this movement and was well connected within the community which helped fuel the philosophies of the Shaw Sisters later in their life.

The Shaw Sisters were born in the Midwest into the upper-middle-class family. When their parents passed away Nicolas went to live with her aunt, Anna Howard Shaw in Pennsylvania. Meanwhile, Eleanor stayed in the Midwest with her husband. While living with her niece, Howard Shaw paid for Nicolas to go to an agricultural school where she met her husband Samuel Fraser. Fraser would go on to be a founder of the Agricultural school at Cornell University which would turn into the College of Agriculture and Life Sciences (CALS). His other large accomplishment was creating a new agricultural technology that would be used to breed new varieties of apples.

While at Cornell University, Fraser became recognized for this new technology and William Wadsworth of Geneseo, New York became very interested in his advancements in agriculture and persuaded both Samuel and Nicolas to come to Geneseo, which is where Nicolas starts to change Livingston County's perception of women. Eleanor's husband died in the early nineteen-tens, and as a result, goes to live temporarily with her sister Nicolas' family in Geneseo. Howard Shaw then takes Eleanor to Budapest to go to an International Women's Convention, in which Nicolas stayed in Geneseo with Eleanor's children. This conference was fundamental in the sister's formation of their feminist ideologies. In 1910, when Eleanor returned to the states, the Shaw Sisters decides to fully settle in Geneseo and start fighting for social reform within suffrage and temperance. Their residence was at 22 main street which is on the North end of the street.

Locomotive, circa 1850's

The Progressive Era sparked an increase in mobility and led many to be able to travel outside their hometowns. Railroads were a key part of that mobility, many carrying passengers to New York City. Coming from the West, many railroads would stop in the center of Geneseo where there was a booming station. This caused Geneseo to be a hub of progressive thinking. Most of Western New York was very conservative, minus the big cities, so Geneseo was full of liberal thinking and action. Along with Eleanor and Nicolas' aunt, Anna influencing their spark in the suffrage movement, the town of Geneseo also played a role in their progressive thinking.

From the early nineteen-teens until the passing of Women's Suffrage in 1919, The Shaw Sisters fought and were active within the community taking on the tradition that had been passed down to them from their aunt and other figures of the movement. Luckily, Geneseo had taken the moniker for the progressive hub from Mount Morris around the same time the sisters settled there. Geneseo was a place that discourse ran freely, and so breaking down barriers within the county was not as complicated as it would have been in a more rural area. They were able to gain traction in the rural communities by holding Saturday night lectures that opened up the conversation of feminism and suffrage in areas they would otherwise not be able to enter.

Despite this, the Shaw Sisters did have adversaries within the community. The grandson of General James S. Wadsworth became a New York Senator and his wife, Alice Hay Wadsworth, both became anti-suffrage. So much so that at the age of thirty-seven Hay Wadsworth became the second president of the anti-suffrage movement, which was founded in 1895, but not a fully formed association until 1911. Splitting their time between Washington DC and the Wadsworth Homestead in Geneseo the Wadsworths never had direct contact with the Shaw Sisters, but there was tension within the community because of the progressives state of the members juxtaposed with the ardent support for the family who started Geneseo.

Their fight with the true anti-suffragist would be subjugated by the people who fear change. Men and women alike were scared of what suffrage and temperance would do for society. When the Women's Movement was initiated, women were not allowed to speak out on any matter. The Culture of Domesticity was the existing set of values that women followed during the mid to late nineteenth century. Women were meant to stay home and take care of the home and family, so them claiming their voice for the first time was able to cause mass hysteria. However, due to Geneseo's progressiveness, the Shaw Sisters became well-respected members of the community that changed public opinion. It was in the rural area that the suffragist needed to persuade the popular opinion

At the dawn of the 1920s, the Women's Movement was accelerating exponentially. In 1915, New York State came close to passing suffrage, but the First World War overshadowed the movement. The following year, Democrats back and fully support the movement. In 1917, New York became the first state in the east to pass suffrage. President Woodrow Wilson would endorse Women's Suffrage in the following year of 1918. This would cause the senate to pass the 19th Amendment in 1919, but it was not truly ratified until August 26th, 1920. Women were to vote following this ratification all due to women like Nicolas and Eleanor Shaw who spent years fighting for what they believed in.

22 Main Street, Geneseo, NY. Home of Nicholas and Eleanor Shaw with Plaque.

The Shaw Sisters would remain active in the community of Geneseo and Livingston County until they died in the late 1940s. When they passed they were still living in their residence of 22 Main Street. In 2018, ninety-nine years after the 19th amendment had passed, the William C Pomeroy Foundation gave a grant to Livingston County Historian, Amie Alden who commemorated their life and contributions with a blue plaque outside of their former residence. Today, people on Main Street can express gratitude for the Shaw Sisters' achievements and the grit they needed to change the local community.

An Afternoon with Amie Alden, Livingston County Historian

On Monday, October 17, we interviewed Livingston County Historian, Amie Alden about her research on the suffragists of Geneseo, specifically the Shaw Sisters. There, we discussed the upbringing of the Shaw Sisters and how they made their way from the Midwest to Western New York under the inspiration of their aunt, Anna Howard Shaw. The Shaw Sisters ended up at Geneseo in 1908 during the suffragist and temperance movements and helped fight for what they believed in. There was a divide between the Wadsworths of Geneseo and the Shaw Sisters due to their beliefs about progression, but there were no direct conflicts. The main goals for the Shaw Sisters differed as Nicholas wanted women to win the right to vote and Eleanor wanted alcohol to be abolished. The Shaw Sisters were considered progressive for their time as they held meetings in town and were part of the Women's Christian Temperance Union.

The Progressive Era had a huge impact on the beliefs of the Shaw Sisters as Geneseo was a hub for different people because it was a stop along several different railroads that ran to New York City. The Shaw Sisters along with Eleanor's children lived in Geneseo until they died. Suffrage meant different things to different individuals in Livingston County. Many of the Men were worried about suffrage and equality due to the inevitable shift in the power dynamic. The suffrage movement in Western New York happened a lot slower than in the City.

Livingston County Historian, Amie Alden and Geneseo Mayor Margaret Duff

The Geneseo Fire Department Memorial

Rachel Mihlstin, Olivia Schoenfeld, Olivia Delahunt

The Geneseo Fire Department is the reason why Geneseo became a town. In order to establish a fire company to protect the village from fires, Geneseo needed to first be recognized as a village. Since its establishment in 1834, the Geneseo Fire Department has been a volunteer company and has grown to acquire better fire truck vehicles; the earliest models were pushcarts and pulled by horses. The fire department was very necessary to the survival of Geneseo as a town because without it, Main Street would not

The Geneseo Fire Department Memorial installation at Temple Hill Cemetery, 1985

have been successfully salvaged from fires so many times. The department's recognition can be seen through the Geneseo landmark.

The Geneseo Fire Department headstone is a landmark that was installed to commemorate the service of its late members. It is in two locations; both cemeteries. The landmark is located in Temple Hill Cemetery. There is also an identical headstone in the St. Mary's Church Cemetery. Its significance for Geneseo can be seen through the recognition of the time that the members spent volunteering. The headstone also honors the families of those who have served. Matt Hutchinson was a volunteer firefighter who passed away in 2016. He is the only member who has died "on duty." While he did not die while putting out a fire, he was an active volunteer firefighter who was very loved by the community. The headstone was erected in 1985 as the fire department was gaining significance. At that time, the community of Geneseo and members of the fire department felt that the town needed to honor this group of people that had kept the community safe for such a long period of time. In order to collect funds, a fundraiser was held. In addition to the main tombstone, bronze grave markers are also placed at their individual graves in order to honor them. Preservation, as always, is extremely important. In this case, the historic preservation is more pertinent than the physical preservation.

The Geneseo Fire Department Memorial Emblem

The Geneseo Fire Department was and continues to be a vital part of the community. Honoring those who have served throughout the years is a great way to acknowledge its significance.

Interview Summary

On September 23rd, 2019 Olivia Delahunt and Rachel Mihlstin met with the Fire Chief Andrew Chanler at Cricket's cafe.

Chanler opened up with sharing his excitement about our interest in this topic. He told us about his role as Fire Chief for the past 15 years and that he has been a part of the Geneseo Fire Department for 32 years. While Fire Chief was his assigned role, Resident Historian was a role he gave himself. It's a passion he has always had. He came prepared and had a powerpoint ready to show us that included all of the work he had found himself while studying the history of the Geneseo Fire Company. He opened with the fact that Geneseo would not be an established town if it was not for the department. They needed to make Geneseo a town because they were plagued with fires and could not get the equipment for a fire company without having a town. So, the village was actually formed in 1832. A petition was sent to the state to incorporate the village.

By late 1832, the town started a basic tax roll and by December, the fire companies began to organize.

After being able to form a fire company, they were able to start protecting the inhabitants. People at this time were very scared of fires because the materials that were used to make buildings and furnish the insides were more flammable than they are today. However, with their new equipment and firefighters, they were able to fight the fires

Photo reel from the Main Street Fire of November 11, 1972

and save Main Street. The first engine house was on Ward Place; back then it was called North Center Street. At the first engine house, they kept a hand pumper. Originally, the hand pumper had to be pulled by a team of horses. From the first team that showed up to the call, the owner would receive a monetary reward.

He goes on to point out a picture of the company at a competition with other departments around the region. There was competition in events like racing up ladders and hitting targets with a hose. Even today, fire departments all over compete in these same competitions.

There used to be a club room above Sweet Arts Bakery for the hose company. Chief Chanler mentioned how there was a bowling alley in the club room. He described how his mother was a pinsetter. Being apart of a club or company was how people socialized back then. Chanler quotes his mother by saying that that is what people did at night before televisions reached the household.

The first motorized piece of equipment was bought in 1992. It was a 1928 Seagrave that was considered a real fire truck. It had a decent size pump on it. The emergency car, which went to rural fires, carried a portable gasoline pump in the back. If there was a fire outside of the village, there would be no water source. So, they might pray for a source from next door but the company would probably not be able to save much. They could stick the portable pump carried by hand in a well and maybe get a stream of water out. But the previous truck was not really set up to do anything outside of the village. Then, they were able to get a custom made engine truck from Rochester.

Even in 1939, the equipment they had was lacking. By the 1940s, there was a first aid squad. The first ambulance, a hearse, was donated by a nearby mortician from Mount Morris. The funeral directors took people to the hospital and if they were tied up, they would have the fire department come and get the person. But then that evolved into a regular ambulance service. There was a rural truck because it had a bigger water tank. In the 1940s, they really did not have helmets or coats. They wore whatever they had that they thought would effectively protect them. The first airpads came into play in 1950 in order to help the firefighters breathe in smoke-ridden situations.

The Geneseo Fire Department Memorial at Temple Hill

Fire on Main Street, November 11, 1972

Chief Chanler went into detail about the changes in equipment, along with various Geneseo fires. Some key fires that were discussed were the 2001 jail fire, the 2000 bus accident, and the 2015 Kelly Saloon fire. Chanler went on to discuss the death of Matt Hutchinson, and how it was very connected to the fire department. Matt volunteered at the fire department. The firehouse was expanded in 2004; basically doubled according to Chanler. Chanler discussed his family background. He described how his family ran a dairy farm and had a route to deliver milk. One consistent part of the Geneseo fire department is that it is all volunteer-based.

Chanler was extremely prepared for this interview. He came bearing a slideshow with various pictures of fires and new fire department equipment in order to give as much information as he could. Chanler said that the history of the fire department is very important to him because "history repeats itself." He believes there is a reason for all of the changes that have been made. An interesting fact regarding the location of the fire station is that its location was chosen because it was cheap to purchase that land.

When asked why the fire department is so important to the town, Chanler spoke about how the department protects the community from fire because fire creeps on us every once in a while. Chanler said that the department has not lost a firefighter in the line of duty. However, members have passed away from illnesses. Chanler believes that this can truly devastate a community. This happened in Avon in 1983, where a firefighter was killed in a fire.

Chanler described some more pictures from his slideshow. Then, Chanler went on to say that the fire history of Geneseo is his passion. When someone asked him about something specific, like the bylaws, he is more than willing to explain the bits and pieces of what happened. The interview with Chanler was extremely helpful in learning more about the history of the fires in Geneseo.

References

Chanler, Andrew. Personal Interview, Sept. 23rd, 2019.

Houston, J. Robert., and Mulligan, William A. A History of the Geneseo Fire Department . Geneseo? N.Y: [Dept.?], 1977. Print.

Smith, Roger B. [Photographs of fire at Scherline's Department Store, Main Street, Geneseo, N.Y.] . N.p., 1972. Print.

Printed in Great Britain
by Amazon

17202628R00022

French Pen [illegible]
Made Easy

A Fun Way to Write French and Make a New Friend

Sinéad Leleu

We hope you and your pupils enjoy corresponding with your French penpals using this book. Brilliant Publications publishes many other books for teaching modern foreign languages in primary schools. To find out more details on any of the titles listed below, please log onto our website: www.brilliantpublications.co.uk.

100+ Fun Ideas for Practising Modern Foreign Languages in the Primary Classroom	978-1-903853-98-6
Chantez Plus Fort!	978-1-903853-37-5
Hexagonie 1	978-1-903853-92-4
Jouons Tous Ensemble	978-1-903853-81-8
C'est Français!	978-1-903853-02-3
J'aime Chanter!	978-1-905780-11-2
J'aime Parler!	978-1-905780-12-9
¡Es Español!	978-1-903853-64-1
Juguemos Todos Juntos	978-1-903853-95-5
¡Vamos a Cantar!	978-1-905780-13-6
Spanish Pen Pals Made Easy	978-1-905780-42-6
Das ist Deutsch	978-1-905780-15-0
Wir Spielen Zusammen	978-1-903853-97-9
German Pen Pals Made Easy	978-1-905780-43-3
Giochiamo Tutti Insieme	978-1-903853-96-2

Published by Brilliant Publications
Unit 10
Sparrow Hall Farm
Edlesborough
Dunstable
Bedfordshire
LU6 2ES, UK

Sales and stock enquiries:
Tel: 01202 712910
Fax: 0845 1309300
E-mail: brilliant@bebc.co.uk
Website: www.brilliantpublications.co.uk

General information enquiries:
Tel: 01525 222292

Written by Sinéad Leleu
Illustrated by James Walmesley
Front cover designed by Gloss Solutions

ISBN 978-1-905780-10-5

First printed and published in the UK in 2008

Contents

Introduction

In this era of technology, we French teachers are spoilt with an excellent array of resource material. Interactive CD-Roms, DVDs, Internet sites … you name it, we use them all. The main aim of all this is that, one day, our pupils will be able to communicate with other French speakers through French. In my own classes, this 'one day' is now. This we do through pen pal correspondence.

My experience has shown me that despite regularly introducing a variety of resources into my classes, rarely a class begins without a pupil asking 'Have our letters arrived yet?' 'Pas encore' is met with disappointment whereas 'Oui' is met with great excitement and delight. My pupils are unwaveringly eager to reply. This may seem like a daunting task to the less confident or the time-strapped teacher but …

For the teacher, ***French Pen Pals Made Easy***:

- does not require fluency
- is time-saving – little or no preparation is required
- links with the KS2 Framework for language teaching
- has inherent cross-curricular links to geography, art and ICT
- supplements, consolidates and revises course work.

For the pupil, ***French Pen Pals Made Easy***:

- is easy to follow. The method used is gap-filling as opposed to giving pupils the daunting task of beginning with a blank page
- is realistic. The pupil realizes that French can be used for real-life communication and not just in an artificial situation
- instils confidence. They can communicate effectively at a basic level
- helps foster positive attitudes towards foreign language learning
- facilitates intercultural understanding. The pupil can learn about French culture through a French peer
- … and, of course, it is fun and a wonderful way to make a new friend. (I should know as I have had the same two pen pals for over 25 years!)

Tips for the teacher

Where to find pen pals

1. There are many websites to help you to find a French-speaking class to correspond with, for example:
   - www.epals.com
   - www.globalgateway.org
   - www.Franceworld.com (click on 'Echange Classes à classes')
   - www.primlangues.fr (click on 'Correspondre')
   - www.etwinning.net
   - www.ipf.net.au (small fee)

   If you have the option of choosing a country, do not forget other countries where you can find French-speaking schools such as Belgium, Luxembourg, Switzerland, Morocco, Tunisia and Canada.

2. If your town is twinned with a French town, you could contact their 'école primaire' (ages 6–10 approx) or 'collège' (ages 11–14 approx).

Checklist for you and your French-speaking counterpart

1. Confirm with your French-speaking counterpart that your pupils will write in French and whether the replies will be in English or French. (They may like to know that ***French Pen Pals Made Easy*** can be purchased from Amazon's French site.)
2. Decide which class will write first.
3. Decide how you are going to pair the pupils. Either one of the teachers decides or the pupils in the class that receives the first letters decide. It is a good idea to make a note of the pairs immediately as some pupils will not remember their pen pal's name. Unless you find a class with the exact same number of pupils, some pupils will have to write two letters.
4. Discuss the expected frequency of your letters. This depends on the school calendar, workload and enthusiasm. Be careful to decide on realistic deadlines. It is a good idea to take one term at a time.
5. Agree on the themes for the term ahead. Take into consideration seasonal events such as Christmas, Hallowe'en and local festivals.

Before pupils begin

1. Before pupils begin to write a letter, it is paramount to have covered the relevant language orally. Remember: **hear it, say it, see it, write it**.

2. Introduce letter writing with a sample letter written on the board, chart or overhead projector. You could use the letter for Unit 1, 'Je me présente', on page 10; this letter can also be downloaded from our website so you can display it on a whiteboard: www.brilliantpublications.co.uk/1010_sample letter.pdf.

Highlight the five main parts of the letter:
- the heading, which includes the town and date
- the greeting
- the body of the letter
- the closing greeting
- the signature

3. Before pupils begin their first letter, explain to them how to use ***French Pen Pals Made Easy***:
   - Point out that pupils must first fill in the blanks and circle where there is a choice.
   - Using imaginary details or those of a pupil in the class, go through the letter line by line. Complete and circle where necessary. See what pupils can come up with themselves before referring to the 'Vocabulaire en plus' section.
   - Write out the entire letter on the board. Explain to pupils that they will need to write a draft into their French workbooks.
   - Tell pupils that you will then correct their draft letters before they write their final letters.

Writing your first letter

1. Having explained how to use ***French Pen Pals Made Easy***, give each pupil the French template letter for 'Je me présente' (page 10). Depending on the class level and time, some teachers will prefer to only give certain sections of the unit. For example, if your class has a good level of French, you may prefer not to hand out the English template. However, if unfinished letters are given as homework, it is advisable to give all four pages of the unit. As the templates and vocabulary are bilingual, parents/guardians will feel comfortable helping.

2. If you give the English template, point out to your pupils that they are not word-for-word translations. It is the ideas that are translated, eg 'There are 25 in my class' is translated to 'Nous sommes 25 dans ma class'. Translated literally, this would be 'We are 25 in my class.'

3. Once you have corrected the pupils' drafts, they should write their letters out neatly to send to their pen pals. Using personalized stationery can help to make their letters special. You can find a variety of stationery online at:
   - www.alapetiteecole.com/papier_a_lettres/
   - www.webmomes.com/pages/lettre.htm
   - www.chezlorry.ca/bricolages.htm

   Allow the pupils to choose for themselves.

4. If pupils wish to include enclosures such as postcards, photos, drawings etc, make sure that they are either stapled or stuck to the letter or that each pupil has their own individual envelope.

As you move on

1. As soon as you receive your first replies, get your pupils to stick their letters into their French workbooks or put them into their French folders.

2. ***French Pen Pals Made Easy*** is flexible so, excepting the first unit (Je me présente), the units may be used in any order.

3. At the beginning of the correspondence, it will be easier for pupils to stick to the template letter. However, as many pupils become more competent, encourage them to change the order of the body of the letter. Weaker pupils can continue to stick to the template letter whereas stronger pupils can use the template letter as a 'springboard'.

4. You can give the class as a whole a choice of topics to choose from. Alternate the choice between the two corresponding classes.

5. To vary the correspondence, you could use other means such as recorded messages on CD, tape, DVD or video.

6. Do not allow pupils to give their home address or telephone number (or email if you are using snail mail) until the correspondence is well established.

Class projects

Class projects are an excellent way to vary class correspondence. The units 'Mon école', 'J'habite!' and 'Noël' are particularly suitable. The projects can be done in English with an English-French glossary. The class can be divided into small groups and given one section each. Include drawings, photos, posters, videos, DVDs, CDs, brochures etc. A class project can be sent along with individual letters or in the place of individual letters. If you have any festivals particular to where you live, this would also be interesting for your pen pals.

Here are some ideas for things that could be included in the class projects:

Mon école

- our class timetable
- after-school activities
- school dinners
- our uniform
- our school building
- our teachers
- our school crest
- history of our school

J'habite

- history
- a map
- landmark(s)
- festivals and celebrations
- clubs / activities for children
- food specialities
- local heroes and / or famous people
- traditional music
- languages and dialect

Noël

- Christmas food
- Christmas tree and decorations
- Christmas crackers
- A typical Christmas carol
- Christmas card-giving tradition (you can find some card-making ideas at: www.teteamodeler.com/dossier/noel/cartesvoeux.asp)
- Christmas stockings and gift-offering tradition
- 12 Days of Christmas
- Pantomimes

Classroom ideas

1. As soon as you receive your first replies, set up a 'pen pal corner' in your classroom. You can include a map of Europe, the world or the country of your pen pals, indicating where they live. You can also make flags of their country and your country. As the correspondence moves along, you can include anything that you or the pupils find interesting such as traditional dishes, school brochures or festivals.

2. To work on oracy skills, pupils can give an oral presentation on their pen pal.

3. As part of art or ICT, pupils can make information sheets based on their pen pals with headings such as:
   - nom
   - âge
   - ville
   - anniversaire
   - couleur des yeux
   - couleur des cheveux
   - frères et sœurs
   - animaux/animal préféré
   - passe-temps
   - couleur préférée
   - musique préférée
   - nourriture préférée
   - boisson préférée
   - matière préférée
   - saison préférée

Tips for the pupil

1. Using a model letter, fill in the blanks and circle the words you would like to use. Check out the '**Vocabulaire en plus**' (Extra vocabulary) section for extra vocabulary. You can keep the English translation nearby to help you.

2. Write out a draft letter (a practice letter). Your teacher will then correct it.

3. Rewrite a final copy of your letter.

4. To make your letter more interesting, use nice stationery and/or decorate your letter with colourful designs and drawings. You can use some of the ideas in the **'Des idées en plus!'** (Extra ideas!) section.

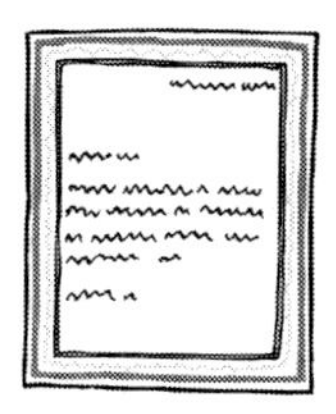

5. Enclose anything you think may interest your pen pal such as stickers, magazine cuttings, and postcards. Again, you will find ideas in the **'Des idées en plus!'** (Extra ideas!) section.

6. **Do not** give your home address, telephone number or home email address without the permission of your parents and teacher.

7. Have fun!

_______________________, le ___________________
(ville/village) (date)

Bonjour!

Je m'appelle ____.

J'ai ____________ ans. Quel âge as-tu?

J'habite à ________________, en / au _______________________.
(ton pays)
Où habites-tu?

Je suis une fille. / Je suis un garçon.

J'aime _________________________ et _______________________.

Je n'aime pas ____.

Au revoir!

____
(ton prénom)

____
(town/village)

____
(date)

Hello!

My name is ______________________________ .

I'm __________ years old. How old are you?

I live in ____________________ , in ____________________ .
(your country)

Where do you live?

I'm a girl. / I'm a boy.

I like ____________________ and ____________________ .

I don't like ______________________________ .

Bye for now!

____
(your first name)

Vocabulaire en plus

Extra vocabulary

le foot	football
le sport	sports
la danse	dancing
le basket	basketball
l'équitation	horse riding
la natation	swimming
l'athlétisme	athletics

le chocolat	chocolate
les bonbons	sweets
le coca	cola
le brocoli	broccoli
la pizza	pizza
les épinards	spinach
les choux de bruxelles	Brussels sprouts
la glace	ice-cream

la musique	rock music
la musique classique	classical music
l'école	school
le cinéma	the cinema
les films d'horreurs	horror movies
la mode	fashion
le théâtre	drama / theatre
Les Simpsons	The Simpsons

(en) France	(in) France
(en) Angleterre	(in) England
(en) Écosse	(in) Scotland
(au) Pays de Galles	(in) Wales
(en) Irlande	(in) Ireland

Points en plus

Extra points

1. Boy or girl?

Your pen pal may not know from your first name if you are a girl or a boy. So, it's a good idea to tell them.

2. J'ai 10 ans

Did you notice that, to say how old we are in French, we say *'J'ai 10 ans'*? This literally means 'I have 10 years'!

3. Le, la, l', les

In English we say:	but in French we say:
I like football.	J'aime **le** foot.
I like ice-cream.	J'aime **la** glace.
I like sweets.	J'aime **les** bonbons.
I like school.	J'aime **l'**école.

le
la
l'
les } the

Le means 'the' before a masculine word such as:

le fromage	the cheese
le brocoli	the broccoli
le jus d'orange	the orange juice

La means 'the' before a feminine word such as:

la glace	the ice-cream
la pomme	the apple
la purée	the mashed potatoes

If a word begins with a vowel (a e i o u), you must use **l'** instead of **le** and **la**. This makes pronunciation easier. So:

l'école	the school
l'équitation	the horse riding
l'athlétisme	the athletics

Les means 'the' before a word in the plural such as:

les pommes	the apples
les chips	the crisps
les bonbons	the sweets

Des idées en plus!

Extra ideas!

Include a map of your country showing where you live. Write *'J'habite ici'* (I live here) and draw an arrow pointing to where you live.

Draw or include pictures of anything that you think is particular to your country such as a double-decker bus or a red postbox.

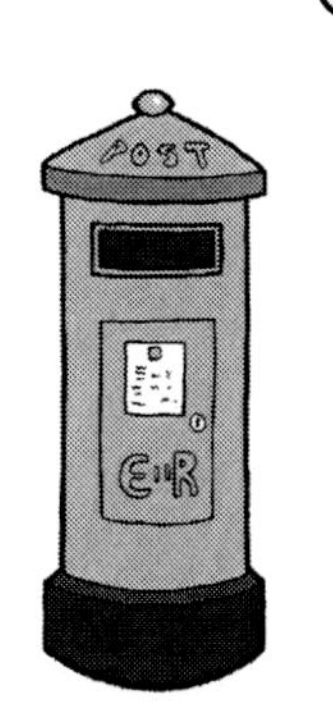

Draw the flag of both your country and your pen pal's country on your letter page. Alternatively, you could draw a page-size flag of your country or your pen pal's country and write your letter on the flag!

Use the colour-by-number flags below to help you.

The United Kingdom Flag

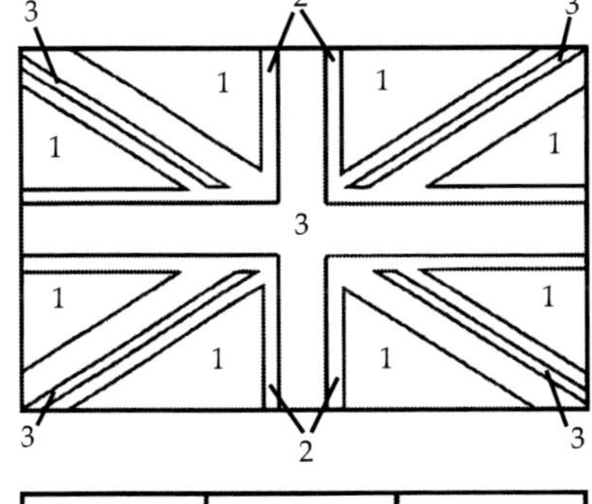

Le drapeau tricolore

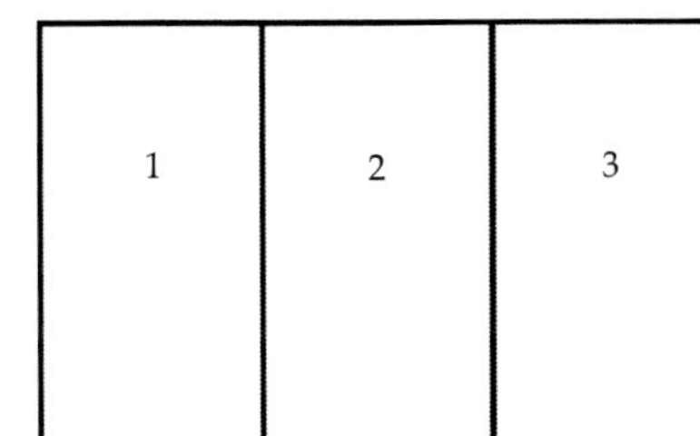

1 = bleu (blue)
2 = blanc (white)
3 = rouge (red)

________________________ , le ____________________
(ville/village) *(date)*

Cher / Chère ____________________ ,

Merci pour ta lettre.

Comment ça va? Moi, ça va ____________________ .

J'ai les yeux ____________________ et les cheveux

________________________ .

Je suis ________________________ et ________________________ .
(adjective) *(adjective)*

Mon anniversaire est le _____ ________________________ .

Quelle est la date de ton anniversaire?

Ma couleur préférée est le ________________________ . Et toi?

Quelle est ta couleur préférée?

Écris-moi vite!

Salut!

____
(ton prénom)

____
(town/village)

____
(date)

Dear ____________________ ,

Thank you for your letter.

How are you? I'm ____________________ .

I have ____________ eyes and ____________ hair.

I'm ____________ *(adjective)* and ____________ *(adjective)* .

My birthday is the ____ of ____________________.
When is your birthday?

My favourite colour is ____________________. How about you?
What's your favourite colour?

Write soon!
Bye!

____
(your first name)

Vocabulaire en plus

Extra vocabulary

bien	well / fine
très bien	very well
pas bien	not well
salut	hi there / bye

bleu	blue
gris	grey
vert	green
jaune	yellow
marron / brun	brown
rose	pink
orange	orange
violet	purple
noir	black
rouge	red
blanc	white

janvier	January
février	February
mars	March
avril	April
mai	May
juin	June
juillet	July
août	August
septembre	September
octobre	October
novembre	November
décembre	December

clair	light
foncé	dark
long	long
court	short
bouclé	curly
raide	straight

sympathique	nice
drôle	funny
aimable	friendly
sensible	sensitive
timide	shy

J'ai les yeux …	
bleus	blue
verts	green
marron	brown
gris	grey
noisettes	hazel
J'ai les cheveux …	
blonds	blonde
châtains	light brown
bruns	dark brown
noir	black
roux	red

Points en plus

Extra points

1. Describing your eyes

In English, we say 'I have green eyes'. The colour comes before the word 'eyes'. Did you notice that in French, the colour comes after the word *'yeux'*? So, *'J'ai les yeux verts'*.

2. Describing your hair

The same is true when describing your hair colour. In English, we say 'I have black hair'. In French, we say *'J'ai les cheveux noirs'*. As *'cheveux'* is plural, we must also make the colour plural. This is usually done by adding *'s'*. The same is true when describing eyes (*'marron'* is an exception). If you want to add a second adjective to describe your hair, you say *'J'ai les cheveux bruns et bouclés'* ('I have brown curly hair').

3. Red hair

The colour 'red' is *'rouge'* in French. However, when we are speaking about 'red hair', we say *'les cheveux roux'*.

4. Writing dates

In English, we write the months with a capital letter, eg the 15th of November. In French, we write the months with a small letter, eg *le 15 novembre*.

5. Colours

When we are saying our favourite colour, we must put *'le'* before the colour, *'Ma couleur préférée est le ___________'*. However, as *'orange'* begins with a vowel, we must put *'l'* before it, *'Ma couleur préférée est l'orange.'*

Des idées en plus!

Extra ideas!

Include a photo of yourself. You can stick it onto the back of your letter and write *'Me voilà!'* ('Here I am!') or *'C'est moi!'* ('It's me').

Me voilà!

Make up some of your own French and English expressions about your new friendship such as:

est
osom
uddies

antastic
unky
riends

mis
miables
musants

harmants
opains
omiques

_______________, le _______________
(ville/village) (date)

Cher / Chère _______________ ,

Merci pour ta lettre et ta photo. Comment ça va?

Moi, ça va bien / très bien / mal.

J'ai ______ sœur(s) et ______ frère(s).

Ma sœur s'appelle _______________ . Elle a ______ ans. /

Mon frère s'appelle _______________ . Il a ______ ans. /

Je suis enfant unique.

Est-ce que tu as des frères et des sœurs?

J'ai un _______________ qui s'appelle _______________ .
(un animal)

Il / Elle est _______________ .
(adjective)

Est-ce que tu as un animal domestique?

Je n'ai pas d'animal domestique, mais mon animal préféré est

le/la _______________ .
(un animal)

Écris-moi vite!

A bientôt! / Salut!

____
(ton prénom)

____
(town/village)

____
(date)

Dear ________________ ,

Thank you for your letter and your photo.

How are you ? I'm fine / very well / not well.

I have ___ sister(s) and ___ brother(s).

My sister's name is ________________ . She is ___ years old. /

My brother's name is ________________ . He is ___ years old. /

I'm an only child.

Do you have brothers and sisters?

I have a ________________ *(animal)* who is called ________________ .

He / she is ________________________ *(adjective)* .

Do you have a pet ?

I don't have a pet, but my favourite animal is the

____________________ *(animal)* .

Write soon!

Talk soon! / Bye!

____
(your first name)

Vocabulaire en plus

Extra vocabulary

Voici	Here is ...
Tu es	You are...
C'est moi	This is me / It's me

mon père	my father
mon papa	my dad
ma mère	my mother
ma maman	my mum
ma belle-mère	my step-mother
mon beau-père	my step-father
mon demi-frère	my step-brother
ma demi-sœur	my step-sister
ma grand-mère	my grandmother
mon grand-père	my grandfather
mes parents d'accueil	my foster parents

un chat	a cat
un chien	a dog
un poisson rouge	a goldfish
un lapin	a rabbit
un hamster	a hamster
un oiseau	a bird
une souris	a mouse
un cheval	a horse
un cochon d'Inde	a guinea pig

sympa	sweet
drôle	funny
pénible	annoying
adorable	adorable
espiègle	playful

Points en plus

Extra points

1. Types of family

There are many types of family. If you live with your grandparents or foster parents or anybody else, you can say *'J'habite avec ___________'* (I live with ___________).

2. Dear ...

If your pen pal is a boy, you must translate 'Dear' to *'Cher'*. If your pen pal is a girl, you must translate 'Dear' to *'Chère'*.

3. More than one brother and sister

For more than one brother, you can say:

Mes frères s'appellent _________ *et* ___________ .
(My brothers' names are _________ and ___________ .)

The same applies for more than one sister:

Mes sœurs s'appellent _________ *et* ___________ .
(My sisters' names are _________ and ___________ .)

4. More than one pet

If you have more than one pet, you can say:

J'ai 2 chiens qui s'appellent __________ *et* __________ .
(I have 2 dogs who are called __________ and __________.)

Don't forget to make the animal plural. Most words are made plural by adding 's', such as:

J'ai 2 poissons rouges, 3 lapins, 4 chats et 5 cochons d'Inde.
(I have 2 goldfish, 3 rabbits, 4 cats and 5 guinea pigs.)

Others have special plural forms, such as:

J'ai 2 oiseaux, 3 souris et 4 chevaux.
(I have 2 birds, 3 mice and 4 horses.)

If you would like to describe your pets, it is easiest to describe each pet individually such as:

J'ai 2 chiens qui s'appellent Max et Molly. Max est espiègle. Molly est adorable.
(I have 2 dogs called Max and Molly. Max is playful. Molly is adorable.)

5. Mon, ma, mes

In French, there are three ways to say 'my':

mon
ma } my
mes

If the noun is masculine, we use '*mon*':	**mon** frère	my brother
If the noun is feminine, we use '*ma*':	**ma** sœur	my sister
If the noun is plural, we use '*mes*':	**mes** frères	my brothers
	mes sœurs	my sisters

Des idées en plus!

Extra ideas!

Include photos of your family. You could stick a photo to the back of your letter. Draw a frame around your photo. Write *'C'est moi'* and use an arrow to point to yourself. For other members of your family, write *'Voici mon frère'* or *'Voici mon beau-père'* etc and use arrows to point to the person in the photo.

________________________ , le ____________________
(ville/village) *(date)*

Salut / Cher / Chère _____________ ,

Merci pour ta lettre / ta photo / tes photos.
Comment ça va? / Comment vas-tu? Moi, ça va bien. / Moi, je vais bien.

As-tu des passe-temps ? Moi, je joue ______________________ /
je fais _____________________ .

J'aime _________________ parce que c'est amusant / relaxant / intéressant / énergétique / un sport d'équipe. Et toi?
Qu'est-ce que tu aimes?

Je collectionne les _____________________ .
En ce moment, je lis '____________________________'.
Je voudrais apprendre à ________________________ .

Dans mon école, le passe-temps le plus populaire est
_______________________ . Et vous?

Ecris-moi vite!
À bientôt! / Ton ami(e),

____
(ton prénom)

____
(town/village)

____
(date)

Hi there / Dear ____________ ,

Thank you for your letter / your photo / your photos.
How are you? / How are you? I'm fine. / I'm fine.

Do you have hobbies? I play ___________________ /
I do ___________________ .

I love _____________ because it's fun / relaxing / interesting / energetic / a team sport. How about you? What do you like?

I collect _____________________ .
At the moment, I'm reading '__________________________'.
I would like to learn to _____________________ .

In my school, the most popular hobby is ____________________ .
How about you?

Write soon!
Talk soon! / Your friend,

____
(your first name)

Vocabulaire en plus

Extra vocabulary

je joue du piano	I play the piano
je joue du violon	I play the violin
je joue de la flûte	I play the flute
je joue de la guitare	I play the guitar

je joue au foot	I play football
je joue au basket	I play basketball
je joue au rugby	I play rugby
je joue au volley	I play volleyball
je joue au hockey	I play hockey
je joue au golf	I play golf

je joue à la playstation	I play on my playstation
je joue à l'ordinateur	I play computer games
je joue à la pétanque/ aux boules	I play petanque/ boules (French games similar to bowls)
je fais du vélo	I cycle
je fais de la gymnastique	I do gymnastics
je fais du judo	I do judo
je fais de l'athlétisme	I do athletics
je fais du karaté	I do karate
je fais de l'équitation	I go horse riding

surtout	especially
et	and
jouer	to play
faire	to do
je n'aime pas	I don't like
je déteste	I hate
j'aime bien	I quite like

la natation	swimming
la lecture	reading
la danse	dancing
nager	to swim
lire	to read
danser	to dance
le dessin	art
le théâtre	theatre
regarder la télé	to watch TV
écouter de la musique	to listen to music
aller au cinéma	to go to the cinema

les timbres	stamps
les poupées	dolls
les autocollants	stickers
les pièces de monnaie	coins
les nounours	cuddly toys
les cartes ________	______ cards

Points en plus

Extra points

1. Sports

jouer à (un sport) – to play (a sport)

In English, when we speak about playing sports we say 'I play football', 'I play volleyball', 'I play hockey', etc.

In French, when the sport is a masculine word, we say:

Je joue **au** foot. I play football.

When the sport is a feminine word, we say:

Je joue **à la** pétanque. I play petanque.

2. Musical instruments

jouer de (un instrument musical) – to play (a musical instrument)
When we speak about playing musical instruments, we say 'I play the piano', I play the guitar', 'I play the violin', etc.

In French when the musical instrument is a masculine word, we say:

Je joue **du** piano.	I play the piano.

When the musical instrument is feminine, we say:

Je joue **de la** guitare.	I play the guitar.

3. J'aime ... – I like ...

You can use the noun or the verb to say you like something:

J'aime la natation.	or	J'aime nager.
J'aime la lecture.	or	J'aime lire.
J'aime le foot.	or	J'aime jouer au foot.
J'aime le piano.	or	J'aime jouer du piano.
J'aime le judo.	or	J'aime faire du judo.

Des idées en plus!

Extra ideas!

Include drawings, photos or magazine cuttings of anything to do with your hobbies, eg your favourite football team, your favourite singers or you practising a hobby.

If you are interested in sports, you could use the caption *'Allez les Bleus!'* (Go the Blues / Come on Blues) along with a football or rugby drawing. *'Allez les Bleus!'* is used to cheer on French teams as they often wear blue.

Mon école!

____________________, le ________________
(ville/village) *(date)*

Cher / Chère ________________ ,

Merci pour ta lettre. / J'étais très content(e) de recevoir ta lettre.
Comment vas-tu ? Moi, je vais bien / très bien / super bien.

Mon école s'appelle __________________________ . C'est une école mixte / de filles / de garçons / pensionnaire. Je suis en ____________ et nous sommes _______ *(nombre)* dans ma classe. Mon professeur / Mon maître / Ma maîtresse s'appelle ____________________ . Il / Elle est ________________________ *(adjective)* .

Je porte un uniforme. / Je ne porte pas d'uniforme. Et toi?

Je fais _______ *(nombre)* matières: ______________________________ *(tes matières)* .
Ma matière préférée est le / la / l' ___________________ parce que c'est ______________________ . Je n'aime pas _______________ parce que c'est _______________ . Quelle est ta matière préférée?

Ecris-moi vite!
Au revoir! / Salut!

____
(ton prénom)

____
(town/village)

____
(date)

Dear _______________ ,

Thank you for your letter. / I was very happy to get your letter.

How are you? I'm fine / very well / great.

My school is called _______________ . It's a mixed / girls' / boys' / boarding school. I'm in year ______ and there are ________ *(number)* in my class. My teacher's name is _______________ . He / She is _______________ *(adjective)* .

I wear a uniform. / I don't wear a uniform. How about you?

I do ________ *(number)* subjects: _______________ *(your subjects)* .

My favourite subject is _______________ because it's _______________ . I don't like _______________ because it's _______________ . What's your favourite subject?

Write soon!

Goodbye! / Bye!

____
(your first name)

Vocabulaire en plus

Extra vocabulary

J'adore	I love
Je déteste	I hate
la récreation	break-time
le déjeuner	lunch

les maths	maths
l'anglais	English
l'histoire	history
la géographie	geography
la musique	music
le sport	PE
le dessin	art
les sciences	science
le français	French
l'éducation civique	citizenship
l'informatique	ICT

lundi	Monday
mardi	Tuesday
mercredi	Wednesday
jeudi	Thursday
vendredi	Friday
samedi	Saturday
dimanche	Sunday

car / parce que	because
c'est	it's
intéressant(e)	interesting
ennuyeux / ennuyeuse	boring
difficile	difficult
facile	easy
gentil(le)	nice
strict(e)	strict
drôle	funny
et	and

Points en plus

Extra points

1. French and British schools

French and British schools have different names for years in school. Find the equivalent for your year.

École Primaire – Primary School

France	UK	Age
CP	Year 2	6
CE1	Year 3	7
CE2	Year 4	8
CM1	Year 5	9
CM2	Year 6	10

Collège – Secondary School

France	UK	Age
6e (sixième)	Year 7	11
5e (cinquième)	Year 8	12
4e (quatrième)	Year 9	13
3e (troisième)	Year 10	14

2. Teacher

'Le professeur' is generally used for secondary school teachers. *'Le maître'* is used for male primary school teachers. *'La maîtresse'* is used for female primary school teachers.

3. Feminine adjectives

If you are describing a girl or woman, you must make the adjective feminine by adding an *'e'* to the adjective:

Il est stict. / Elle est stricte. He is strict. / She is strict.

If the adjective already ends with an *'e'*, we do not add an extra *'e'*.

4. C'est + adjective

The adjective remains unchanged following *'c'est'*. Even if *'c'est'* refers to a feminine noun, the adjective does not agree with it.

Il est intéressant.
Elle est intéressante. } C'est intéressant.

5. Ton, ta, tes

In French, there are three ways to say 'your':

ton
ta
tes } your

If the noun is masculine, we use *'ton'*:	**ton** déjeuner	your dinner
If the noun is feminine, we use *'ta'*:	**ta** matière	your subject
If the noun is plural, we use *'tes'*:	**tes** professeurs	your teachers

If a noun is feminine and starts with a vowel (a e i o u), we use *'ton'* as this makes pronunciation easier, eg *'ton école'* (your school).

Des idées en plus!

Extra ideas!

Include your own timetable. Write each subject in a different colour. If you don't have a timetable, ask your teacher. Here is an example to help you do your own: *'Voici mon emploi du temps'* ('Here is my timetable').

	9h15	9h45	10h15		11h20	12h20		14h	14h30	15h	15h30
lundi	Maths	Dessin		Récréation	Dessin		Déjeuner	Français	Anglais		Géographie
mardi	Anglais	Maths			Sciences			Sciences	Géographie		Anglais
mercredi	Histoire	Maths			Anglais	Informatique		Informatique	Sciences		Sport
jeudi	Français	Sport			Musique			Éducation civique	Maths	Anglais	Maths
vendredi	Sciences	Sport			Histoire			Éducation civique	Maths		Anglais

____________________ , le ________________
(ville/village) *(date)*

Cher / Chère __________ ,

Merci pour ta lettre. / J'étais très content(e) de recevoir ta lettre.
J'espère que tu vas bien. Moi, je vais bien / pas mal / super bien.

Qu'est-ce que tu aimes manger? Moi, j'aime le / la / les
________________ et __________________ .
Je n'aime pas le / la / les __________________ .

Qu'est-ce que tu aimes boire? Moi, j'aime le / la
________________ et le / la ________________ .
Je n'aime pas le / la __________________ .

Ici en/au ________________ , '____________________'
(ton pays)
est un plat traditionnel.

Ecris-moi vite!
Ton ami(e),

____
(ton prénom)

____
(town/village)

____
(date)

Dear ______________ ,

Thank you for your letter. / I was very happy to get your letter.
I hope you are well. I'm fine / not bad / great.

What do you eat? I like ______________ and
______________ .
I don't like ______________ .

What do you like to drink? I like ______________ and
______________ .
I don't like ______________ .

Here in ______________ , '______________'
(your country)
is a traditional dish.

Write soon!
Your friend,

____
(your first name)

Vocabulaire en plus

Extra vocabulary

le café	coffee
le thé	tea
le coca	cola
le jus d'orange	orange juice
le lait	milk
l'eau	water
le chocolat chaud	hot chocolate

la glace à la vanille	vanilla ice-cream
la glace au caramel	caramel ice-cream
la glace à la fraise	strawberry ice-cream
les bonbons	sweets
la crème anglaise	custard
les crêpes	pancakes
le gâteau	cake
le chocolat	chocolate

l'ananas	pineapple
la framboise	raspberry
l'orange	orange
les raisins	grapes
la banane	banana
la pomme	apple
les raisins secs	raisins

le sandwich au fromage	cheese sandwich
le sandwich au jambon	ham sandwich
la purée	mashed potatoes
l'omelette	omelette
la soupe	soup
les frites	chips
la pizza	pizza
la quiche	quiche
les chips	crisps
le steak haché	burger

les pommes de terre	potatoes
la carotte	carrot
le brocoli	broccoli
les épinards	spinach
la salade	salad
les choux de bruxelles	Brussels sprouts

j'adore	I love
j'aime bien	I quite like
je déteste	I hate
Miam, miam!	Yum, yum!
Beurk!	Yuck!

Points en plus

Extra points

1. Your friend

'Ton ami' or *'ton amie'*? If you are a boy, you say *'ton ami'*. If you are a girl, you say *'ton amie'*. We add on an *'e'* to *'amie'* to make *'ami'* feminine.

2. French dishes

It is true that in France, *'des cuisses de grenouilles'* (frogs' legs) and *'des escargots'* (snails) are dishes. They are, however, quite rare. You could ask your pen pal if he or she has ever tasted them:

As-tu déjà goûté aux cuisses de grenouilles ou aux escargots?
(Have you ever tasted frogs' legs or snails?)

Des idées en plus!

Extra ideas!

Include the recipe for the traditional dish you have chosen. You can write this in English but look up the ingredients in a bilingual dictionary and include a mini-glossary.

Design your perfect menu. Put it on the back of your letter. Use the example below to help you.

Voice le menu idéale!
(Here is the ideal menu!)

Ma journée!

_________________________ , le _____________________
(ville/village) *(date)*

Salut! / Cher / Chère ________________ ,

J'étais ravi(e) de recevoir ta lettre. Merci beaucoup.
Comment vas-tu? Moi, je vais bien / super bien.

Comment se passe ta journée? Moi, je me lève à ______________ .
À quelle heure tu te lèves? L'école commence à ____________. Et ton école?

Je déjeune à ____________ et je quitte l'école à ____________ . Et toi?

Je dîne à ____________ et je me couche à ___________ . À quelle heure tu te couches?

Quelle est ta saison préférée? Moi, ma saison préférée est __________________ parce que j'adore ____________________ et quand il __________________________________ .
(le temps)

Ecris-moi vite!
À bientôt! / Salut!

____
(ton prénom)

____
(town/village)

____
(date)

Hi there! / Dear ____________ ,

I was deighted to get your letter. Thank you very much.
How are you? I'm fine / great.

How is your day? I get up at _______ a.m. What time do you get up? School starts at _________ a.m. What about your school?

I have lunch at __________ p.m. and I leave school at __________ p.m. How about you?

I have dinner at ___________ and I go to bed at __________ .
What time do you go to bed?

What's your favourite season? My favourite season is _________________ because I love ____________________
and when it ___________________________ .
(the weather)

Write soon!
Talk soon! / Bye!

____
(your first name)

Vocabulaire en plus

Extra vocabulary

je mange le petit déjeuner	I eat breakfast
je quitte la maison	I leave home
j'arrive à l'école	I get to school
je dors	I sleep
je fais des activités extra-scolaires	I do after-school activities
je regarde la télé	I watch TV
je lis	I read

il fait beau	it's fine
il fait du soleil	it's sunny
il neige	it's snowing
il fait du vent	it's windy
il fait chaud	it's hot
il pleut	it's raining
il fait froid	it's cold

le printemps	spring
l'été	summer
l'automne	autumn
l'hiver	winter

Noël	Christmas
les vacances scolaires	the school holidays
Halloween	Hallowe'en
Les vacances de Pâques	Easter holidays
mon anniversaire	my birthday
aller à la plage	to go to the beach
les couleurs d'automne	autumn colours
les jonquilles	the daffodils
faire un bonhomme de neige	to make a snowman
faire une bataille de boules de neige	to have a snowball fight

Des idées en plus!

Extra ideas!

Time

In English, we usually use a.m. and p.m. to differentiate between morning and evening. In French, it is more common to use the 24 hour clock.

1 a.m. = 1h	7 a.m. = 7h	1 p.m. = 13h	7 p.m. = 19h
2 a.m. = 2h	8 a.m. = 8h	2 p.m. = 14h	8 p.m. = 20h
3 a.m. = 3h	9 a.m. = 9h	3 p.m. = 15h	9 p.m. = 21h
4 a.m. = 4h	10 a.m. = 10h	4 p.m. = 16h	10 p.m. = 22h
5 a.m. = 5h	11 a.m. = 11h	5 p.m. = 17h	11 p.m. = 23h
6 a.m. = 6h	12 p.m. = 12h	6 p.m. = 18h	12 a.m. = 24h

In French, the minutes go after the h (the hour), so:

8.15 a.m. = 8h15

8.30 a.m. = 8h30

8.45 a.m. = 8h45

Points en plus

Extra points

Fill in the times in the following daily routine.

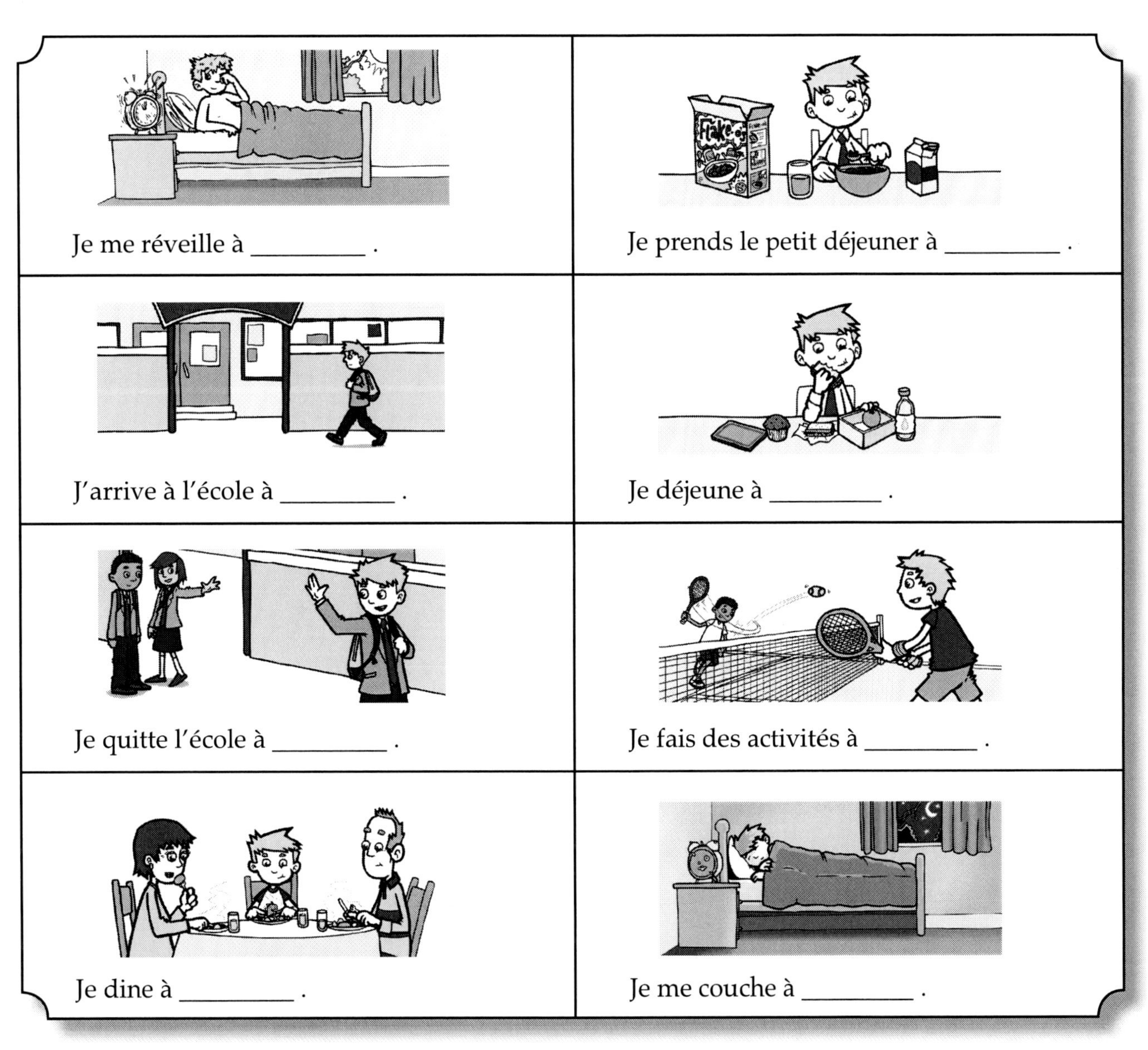

Je me réveille à ________ .	Je prends le petit déjeuner à ________ .
J'arrive à l'école à ________ .	Je déjeune à ________ .
Je quitte l'école à ________ .	Je fais des activités à ________ .
Je dine à ________ .	Je me couche à ________ .

To make your daily routine more interesting, why not add speech bubbles.
You could fill them with comments such as:

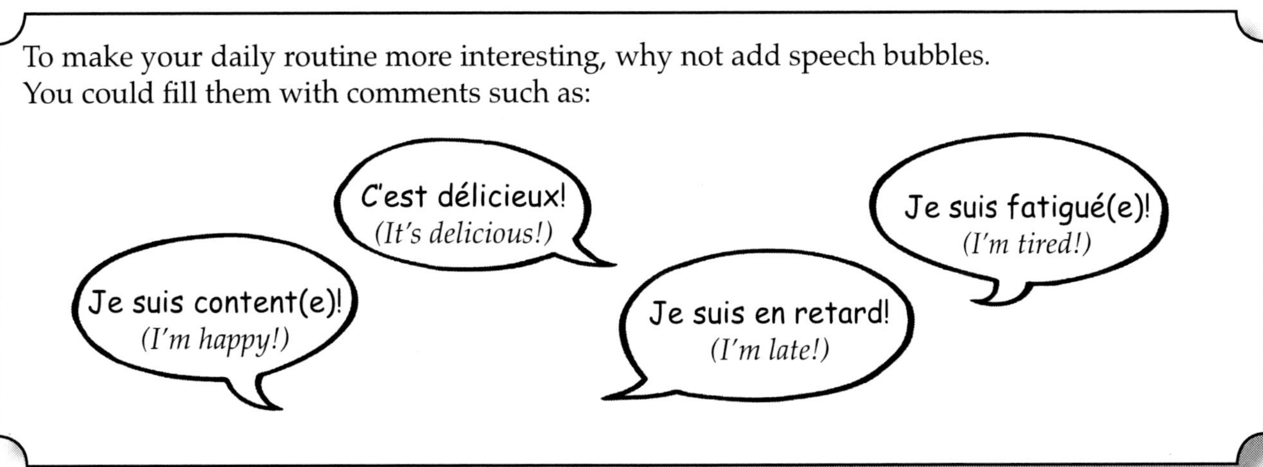

_______________ , le _______________
(ville/village) *(date)*

Bonjour / Cher / Chère _______________ ,

Comment vas-tu?

Je vais bien, merci. / Je vais super bien, merci.

J'habite à _____________ . C'est un village / une ville / une grande ville / à la campagne. C'est _______________ *(adjectif)* .
Il y a ________ habitants. Comment est ta ville / ton village?

À _______________ *(ta ville/ton village)* , il y a une piscine / une bibliothèque / un supermarché / un hôpital / une mairie / un café / un restaurant / un cinéma / une école / un parc / une pharmacie / un boucher / une boulangerie / un château / une rivière / une église.

Chaque année au mois de _______________ , nous fêtons _______________ *(coutume/tradition)* / nous avons une fête foraine. Et vous?

Écris-moi vite!

Au revoir! / Salut!/ Ton ami(e),

____
(ton prénom)

____
(town/village)

____
(date)

Hello / Dear ____________________ ,

How are you?
I'm fine, thanks. / I'm great, thanks.

I live in ___________________ . It's a village / a town / a city / in the country. It's _______________________ *(adjective)* . There are ______ inhabitants. What's your town / your village like?

In ____________________ *(your town/ village)* , there is a swimming pool / a library / a supermarket / a hospital / a town hall / a café / a restaurant / a cinema / a school / a park / a pharmacy / a butcher / a bakery / a castle / a river / a church.

Every year in the month of __________________, we celebrate ___________________________________ *(custom/tradition)* / we have a carnival.
How about you?

Write soon!
Goodbye! / Bye! / Your friend,

____
(your first name)

Vocabulaire en plus

Extra vocabulary

une banque	a bank
un stade	a stadium
un magasin	a shop
un musée	a museum
la poste	the post office
un marché	a market
une patinoire	an ice-rink
une rue	a street
une gare	a train station
un aéroport	an airport
une usine	a factory

animé(e)	busy
grand(e)	big
bruyant(e)	noisy
joli(e)	pretty
tranquille	peaceful
petit(e)	small
beau/belle	beautiful /nice
sympa	nice
calme	calm
ennuyeux/ennuyeuse	boring
vivant(e)	lively

sur	on
une île	an island
au bord de la mer	by the seaside
près de	near

une kermesse	a fair
la nouvelle année chinoise	the Chinese New Year
La Saint-George	Saint George's Day
Mardi Gras	Pancake Day
La Saint-André	Saint Andrew's Day
la Fête du travail	May Day
le défilé de Pâques	the Easter parade

Points en plus

Extra points

1. Prepositions to describe where you live

You can give a clearer idea of where you live by using prepositions, for example:

C'est près de Leeds / Manchester / Londres / Stonehenge.
(It's near Leeds / Manchester / London / Stonehenge.)

C'est au bord de la mer.
(It's by the seaside.)

C'est sur une île.
(It's on an island.)

C'est sur Île de ________.
(It's on the Isle of _________.)

2. Adjectives

You can also use adjectives to describe buildings and public places. Don't forget that adjectives often go before the noun in French. For example:

un beau musée	a nice museum
une belle piscine	a nice swimming pool
un grand stade	a big stadium
une grande église	a big church

3. Plurals

In French, *'un'* and *'une'* become *'des'* in the plural. We usually put an *'s'* on the end of the noun to make it plural. For example:

Il y a **un** restaurant.	There is a restaurant.
Il y a **des** restaurant**s** .	There are restaurants.
Il y a **une** banque.	There is a bank.
Il y a **des** banque**s**.	There are banks.

4. Famous for anything?

If the area where you live is famous or known for anything such as a market, a sporting event, a famous person, a particular type of food or an historical event, you can say:

________________ *est connu pour* ________________ .
(ta ville)

(________________ is famous/known for ____________ .)
(your town)

Des idées en plus!

Extra ideas!

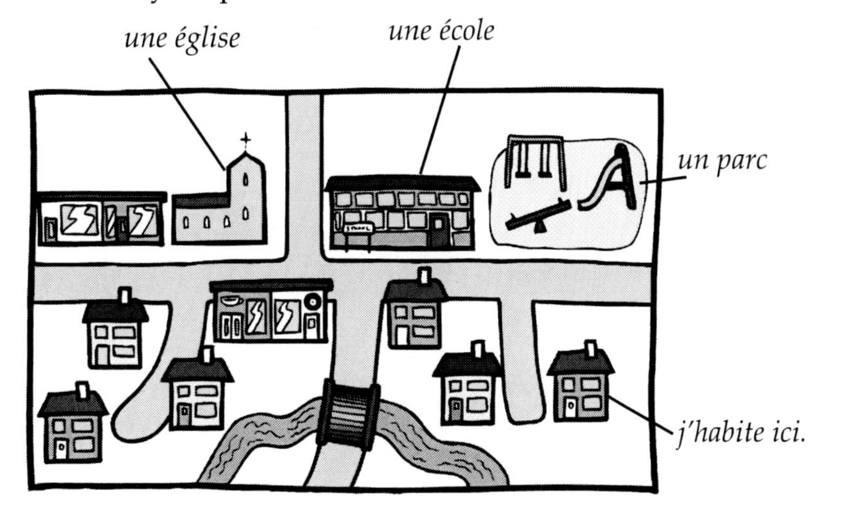

____________________ , le ________________
(ville/village) *(date)*

Salut / Bonjour / Cher / Chère __________________ ,

Comment vas-tu? Moi, je vais bien / pas bien.
Merci beaucoup pour ta lettre.

Tu aimes la mode? Moi, j'adore / je déteste la mode.

Le week-end, j'aime porter ______________ et ______________ .
J'aime les vêtements ______________________ . Et toi?
(adjective)

Je porte un uniforme à l'école. C'est obligatoire. / Je ne porte pas d'uniforme. Tu portes un uniforme?

Je porte un pull ________________ *(couleur)* / un pantalon _______________ *(couleur)* / une chemise _______________ *(couleur)* / une jupe ___________ *(couleur)* / une robe ____________ *(couleur)* / une cravate __________ *(couleur)* / un survêtement ______________ *(couleur)* / des chaussettes __________ *(couleur)* .
______________________________ *(adjective)*, n'est-ce pas!

Ecris-moi vite!
Ton ami(e) / Bye! / Bisous!

____
(ton prénom)

____
(town/village)

____
(date)

Hi / Hello / Dear ____________________ ,

How are you? I'm fine / not well.
Thanks a lot for your letter.

Do you like fashion? I love /hate fashion.

At the weekend, I like to wear __________________ and
______________ . I like _____________ clothes. How about you?
(adjective)

I wear a uniform to school. It's compulsory. / I don't wear a uniform. Do you wear a uniform?

I wear a _____________ jumper / _____________ trousers / a
(colour) *(colour)*
_____________ shirt / a _____________ skirt / a
(colour) *(colour)*
_____________ dress / a _____________ tie / a
(colour) *(colour)*
_____________ tracksuit / _____________ socks.
(colour) *(colour)*
___________________________ , isn't it!
(adjective)

Write soon!
Your friend / Salut! / Love

____
(your first name)

Vocabulaire en plus

Extra vocabulary

grand	big
petit	small
long	long
court	short
démodé	old-fashioned

rouge	red
orange	orange
jaune	yellow
vert	green
rose	pink
bleu	blue
violet	purple
noir	black
marron	brown
blanc	white
gris	grey
bleu marine	navy

un jean	jeans
un t-shirt	a t-shirt
un sweat	a sweatshirt
des baskets	trainers
une robe	a dress
une écharpe	a scarf
une casquette	a cap
une veste	a jacket
un bonnet	a hat
un manteau	a coat
un chemisier	a blouse
un maillot	a jersey

à la mode	fashionable
branché	trendy
ringard	old-fashioned
confortable	comfortable
simple	simple
à couleur vive	brightly coloured
joli	lovely
affreux	awful

d'habitude	usually
parfois	sometimes

Points en plus

Extra points

1. Adjective agreement

Colours are adjectives, so they need to agree with the noun they are describing.

If the noun is masculine, you need to use the masculine form of the colour:

un pull **bleu**	a blue jumper
un pantalon **vert**	a pair of green trousers

If the noun is feminine, you need to use the feminine form of the colour:

une veste **bleue**	a blue jacket
une jupe **verte**	a green dress

Exceptions
If the colour already ends with '*e*', you do not add another '*e*', eg '*rouge*'.
'Violet' becomes 'violette' in the feminine.
'Long' becomes 'longue' in the feminine.

If the noun is plural, you must add '*s*' to the colour:

des pulls bleu**s**	some blue jumpers
des pantalons vert**s**	some pairs of green trousers
des chaussettes grise**s**	some grey shoes
des chaussures noire**s**	some black shoes

2. Bisous

French children often use '*bisous*' as their closing greeting. It literally means 'kisses'. The English equivalent for a closing greeting would probably be 'love'.

Des idées en plus!

Extra ideas!

Ma tenue préfèrée (My favourite outfit)
Draw your favourite outfit on your letter or include a photo of you wearing your favourite outfit, sports gear or uniform.

Chez moi!

____________________ , le ________________
(ville/village) *(date)*

Bonjour / Cher / Chère __________________ ,

Merci pour ta lettre. J'étais très content(e) de la recevoir.
J'espère que tu vas bien.

J'habite dans un / une ____________________ . Il y a
(genre de maison)
______ pièces. Il y a ________________ , __________________ ,
__________________ et __________________ .

J'ai ma propre chambre. / Je partage ma chambre avec
________________________ . Dans ma chambre, il y a
________________ , _________________ et _______________ .

Nous avons aussi un ________________ jardin /balcon avec
__________________ .

Écris-moi bientôt et décris-moi ta maison!

Salut! / À bientôt /Ton ami(e),

____
(ton prénom)

____
(town/village)

____
(date)

Hello / Dear ______________________ ,

Thank you for your letter. I was delighted to get it.
I hope you are well.

I live in a / an ______________________ . There are _____ rooms.
(type of house)
There is ________________ , ________________ , ________________
and ____________________ .

I have my own bedroom. / I share my bedroom with
_____________________ . In my bedroom, there is ______________ ,
____________________ and __________________ .

We also have a _________________ garden / balcony with
________________________ .

Write soon and describe your house!

Bye! / Talk soon! / Your friend,

____
(your first name)

Vocabulaire en plus

Extra vocabulary

une cave	a cellar
une cuisine	a kitchen
un salon	a sitting-room
une chambre	a bedroom
un bureau	an office
une salle de jeux	a playroom
une véranda	a conservatory
une salle de bains	a bathroom
un grenier	an attic
un garage	a garage
une salle à manger	a dining room

un lit	a bed
une table de nuit	a bedside table
une télé	a TV
une télévision	a television
une armoire	a wardrobe
un tapis	a rug
un lecteur de CD	a CD player
une commode	a chest of drawers
un poster	a poster
une étagère	a shelf

ma sœur	my sister
mes sœurs	my sisters
mon frère	my brother
mes frères	my brothers

grand	big
petit	small
une fleur	a flower

des balançoires	swings
un arbre	a tree
un panier de basket	a basketball ring

une maison	a house
un appartement	an apartment
une caravane	a caravan
une habitation flottante	a houseboat

Points en plus

Extra points

1. Plurals

If you have more than one of a certain room or piece of furniture, do not forget to make the noun plural. For example:

Il y a une chambre. — There is 1 bedroom.
Il y a 4 chambres. — There are 4 bedrooms.

Il y a un poster. — There is a poster.
Il y a des posters. — There are posters.

2. 1 or a

The number '1' and the word 'a' are both translated into '*un*' or '*une*', so

There is 1 bedroom. There is a bedroom.	Il y a une chambre.
There is 1 poster. There is a poster.	Il y a un poster.

Des idées en plus!

Extra ideas!

Include a photo or drawing of your house or apartment block.

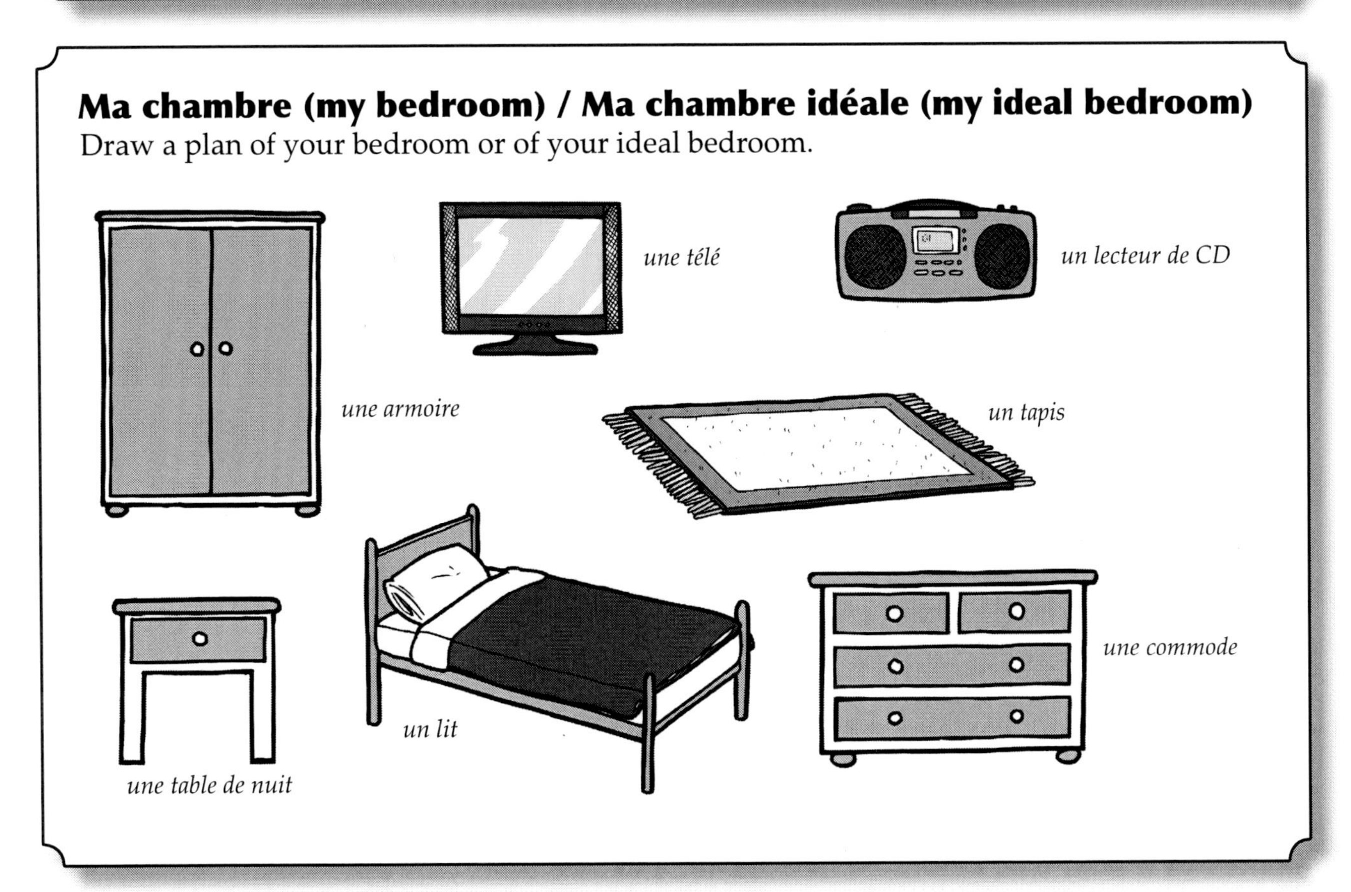

____________________ , le __________________
(ville/village) *(date)*

Cher / Chère ____________________ ,

Merci beaucoup pour ta lettre. / J'étais très content(e) de recevoir ta lettre.

J'espère que tu vas bien. Moi, je vais bien / très bien / super bien.

J'adore / J'aime Noël. Et toi?

En/Au ________________ *(ton pays)* beaucoup de familles fêtent Noël. Les enfants laissent des chaussettes sur la cheminée. Le Père Noël laisse les cadeaux dedans.

Le jour de Noël, je dîne avec __________________ . Nous mangeons _______________ . Et vous? Après manger, nous tirons des 'crackers'.

Ce Noël, je voudrais __________________________ *(un cadeau)* . Et toi?

Joyeux Noël et Bonne Année!
Ton ami(e),

____
(ton prénom)

____
(town/village)

____
(date)

Dear ____________________ ,

Thank you for your letter. / I was very happy to get your letter.

I hope you are well. I'm fine / very well / great.

I love / I like Christmas. How about you?

In ________________ *(your country)* many families celebrate Christmas. The children leave stockings on the chimney. Father Christmas leaves presents in them.

On Christmas Day, I have dinner with ______________ . We eat ______________ . How about you? After dinner, we pull 'crackers'.

This Christmas, I would like ________________ *(a present)*. How about you?

Merry Christmas and Happy New Year!
Your friend,

____
(your first name)

Vocabulaire en plus

Extra vocabulary

La veille de Noël	Christmas Eve
la crèche	the crib
une bûche de Noël	a Christmas log
un sapin de Noël	a Christmas tree
des décorations	decorations
des guirlandes	tinsel
une étoile	a star

un skate	a skateboard
un jeu vidéo	a video game
un ordinateur	a computer
un CD	a CD
un portable	a mobile phone
un vélo	a bike
des patins à roulettes	roller blades
un livre	a book
un DVD	a DVD

ma mère	my mother
mon père	my father
ma sœur	my sister
mon frère	my brother
mes grandparents	my grandparents
mes cousins	my cousins

en Angleterre	in England
en Irlande	in Ireland
en Écosse	in Scotland
au Pays de Galles	in Wales

de la dinde	turkey
des pommes de terre rôties	roast potatoes
des carottes	carrots
des choux de Bruxelles	Brussels sprouts
un 'mince pie' (tartelette à la pâte de fruits secs)	a mince pie
un 'Christmas pudding' (gâteau aux fruits secs)	a Christmas pudding

Points en plus

Extra points

1. Christmas cards

In France, people don't usually send Christmas cards. They sometimes send cards to wish a Happy New Year.

2. Stockings or shoes?

In France, children don't leave out stockings at Christmas. They leave their shoes under the Christmas tree. Père Noël (Father Christmas) leaves the presents next to the shoes.

3. Crackers

Pulling crackers is not a French tradition.

Des idées en plus!

Extra ideas!

Although it is not tradition in France to send Christmas cards, it would be interesting for your French pen pal to learn about your tradition of sending Christmas cards. You could make a card and write a greeting such as:

Joyeux Noël et Bonne Année
(Merry Christmas and Happy New Year)

As most French people don't usually know about Christmas crackers, you could make one for your pen pal. You will need:

- a toilet paper roll
- crêpe paper
- a ribbon
- goodies such as sweets, a paper hat, a small toy

Don't put a snapper in as it is illegal to post them overseas.

Instructions:

- Fill the roll with some goodies.
- Wrap the roll in the crêpe paper.
- Gather the crêpe paper at both ends of the roll and tie with the ribbon.
- As your pen pal may not know what to do with the cracker, include the following instructions:

> *Deux personnes tiennent une extrémité chacun et ils tirent. La personne qui a le plus grand morceau a le droit de garder le contenu.*
>
> (Two people hold an end each and pull. The person with the biggest piece gets to keep the content.)

Les grandes vacances!

________________________ , le ____________________
(ville/village) *(date)*

Cher / Chère ________________ / Salut!

Merci pour ta lettre. / J'ai adoré ta lettre. Merci!

Les grandes vacances approchent. ____________________ !

Quand je pense aux vacances, je pense au / à la / à l' /aux

__________________ , ______________________ et

_______________________ . Et toi? À quoi tu penses?

Au mois de _______________________ , je vais aller
(le mois)

____ avec
(dans un pays/ à une ville)

__________________________ / je vais me reposer à la maison.

Et toi? Tu pars en vacances?

Je vais aussi ______________________________________ .
(faire une activité)

Qu'est-ce que tu vas faire cet été?

Aujourd'hui, il ____________________ . Quel temps fait-il chez toi?

Ecris-moi vite!

A bientôt!/ Ton ami(e),

____
(ton prénom)

____
(town/village)

____
(date)

Dear ______________ / Hi!

Thank you for your letter. / I loved your letter. Thank you!

The summer holidays are coming. ______________ !

When I think of the holidays, I think of ______________ , ______________ and ______________ . How about you? What do you think of?

In ______________ , I'm going
(month)

______________________ with
(to a country/ a town)

______________ / I'm going to relax at home.

How about you? Are you going on holiday?

I'm also going to ______________________ . What are you going to do this summer?
(do an activity)

Today, it's ______________ . What's the weather like over there?

Write soon!

Talk soon! / Your friend,

____
(your first name)

Vocabulaire en plus

Extra vocabulary

Chouette!	Great!
Génial!	Fantastic!
Formidable!	Wonderful!
Youpi!	Yippee!

aller à un centre aéré	to go to a summer camp
aller en colonie de vacances	to go to a holiday camp

la plage	beach
le soleil	sun
la grasse-mâtinée	lie-in
le château de sable	sandcastle
la mer	the sea
le pique-nique	picnic
la glace	ice-cream

jouer au foot	to play football
jouer au basket	to play basketball
faire des cours de français	to do French classes
faire du cheval	to go horse riding
faire des jeux	to play games
faire du camping	to go camping

ma famille	my family
mes parents	my parents
mes grandparents	my grandparents
mes cousins	my cousins

il fait beau	it's fine
il fait du soleil	it's sunny
il pleut	it's raining
il fait chaud	it's hot
il fait froid	it's cold
il fait du vent	it's windy

Points en plus

Extra points

1. Penser à: au, à la, à l', aux

If you want to say, 'I think of ________', you say *'je pense à ________'*. We know that *le*, *la*, *l'* and *les* all mean 'the'. The word *'à'* changes with some forms of 'the':

For example:

à + le = au	Je pense **au** soleil.
à + la = à la	Je pense **à la** plage.
à + l' = à l'	Je pense **à l'**été.
à + les = aux	Je pense **aux** pique-niques.

2 Aller à: to go to

If you are going to a town, you simply say:

Je vais à Blackpool.
(I'm going to Blackpool.)

Je vais à Bournemouth.
(I'm going to Bournemouth.)

If you are going to a country that begins with a vowel or that is feminine, you say:

*Je vais **en** Écosse.*
(I'm going to Scotland.)

*Je vais **en** Belgique.*
(I'm going to Belgium.)

If you are going to a country that is masculine, you say:

*Je vais **au** Portugal.*
(I'm going to Portugal.)

*Je vais **au** Pays de Galles.*
(I'm going to Wales.)

Des idées en plus!

Extra ideas!

Include a map of Europe. Use arrows to point to countries you would like to visit:

Voici les pays où j'aimerais bien visiter.
(Here are the countries I would like to visit.)

If you have visited some of these countries, you can say:

Voici les pays où je suis allé(e).*
(Here are the countries I have visited.)

*If you are girl, you must add '*e*'.